AGAINST ALL ODDS

BREAKING THE POVERTY TRAP

HARRY BHASKARA
DARRYL D'MONTE
NURUL HUDA
JOHN MUKELA
DOROTHY MUNYAKHO
ANTHONY NGAIZA
WINNIE OGANA
USHA RAi
MALLIKA WANIGASUNDARA

with

DONATUS DE SILVA

AGAINST ALL ODDS

INDIA: The pavement dwellers of Bombay
Text and photographs by Darryl D'Monte

TANZANIA: A life-saving clinic in remote Chanika
Text by Anthony Ngaiza. Photographs by Bwire Musalika

BANGLADESH: Breaking the grip of greedy landowners
Text by Nurul Huda. Photographs by Moazzem Hossain Bulu

KENYA: The parking boys of Nairobi
Text by Dorothy Munyakho. Photographs by Owile Ndeko

INDIA: No longer need they abandon home
Text by Usha Rai. Photographs by Nitin Rai

KENYA: The water that brings new life
Text by Winnie Ogana. Photographs by Sam Ouma

SRI LANKA : Growing trees in the light of the Buddha
Text by Mallika Wanigasundara. Photographs by Rohini de Mel

ZAMBIA: The same hands, but new minds
Text and photographs by John Mukela

INDONESIA: Ending the daily water chore
Text and photographs by Harry Bhaskara

Project Co-ordinator: Donatus de Silva

© The Panos Institute 1989
All rights reserved

Published by Panos Publications Ltd
8 Alfred Place
London WC1E 7EB
UK

First published 1989

British Library Cataloguing in Publication Data:
Against All Odds: Breaking the poverty trap
1. Community action.
I. Title II de Silva, Donatus
361.8
ISBN 1-870670-10-8

Extracts may be freely reproduced by the press or by non-profit
organisations, with or without acknowledgement. Panos would appreciate
clippings of published material based on *Against All Odds*.

Any judgments expressed in this document should not be taken to
represent the views of the Panos Institute or any of its funding agencies.

The Panos Institute is an international information and policy studies
institute, dedicated to working in partnership with others towards greater
public understanding of sustainable development. Panos has offices in
London, Paris and Washington DC, and was founded in 1986 by the staff
of Earthscan, which had undertaken similar work since 1975.

For more information about Panos contact: James Deane, Press Officer

Editorial Director: Benjamin Pogrund, assisted by Sue Bretherton and
Naella Denby
Production: Matthew Rake, Jacqueline Walkden
Publications director: Liz Carlile
Photo research: Patricia Lee
Graphic design: Veridian, London
Maps: Philip Davies

Printed in Great Britain by Camelot Press, Southampton.

This book is dedicated to the hundreds of citizens' groups throughout the world, who are battling against all odds

Against All Odds is published as part of the Panos Focal Country Programme, which is funded by SIDA, DANIDA, FINNIDA, the Norwegian Ministry of Development Co-operation, and the Netherlands Ministry of Foreign Affairs.

INTRODUCTION

"The project has freed me from the chains of money-lenders by enabling me to earn more. I used to borrow money by mortgaging family brassware items at very high rates of interest — simply to meet the costs of basic necessities. There used to be no escape from the money-lenders after my family had spent days with no food to eat at all." — **Rabindranath, a small farmer in Bangladesh.**

"I gathered scattered potatoes at the 'marikiti' (market) and sold them, I unscrewed the lamps on people's cars and sold them. I pounced on women at night and snatched their money and anything else they had." — **Muhoro, a former destitute Kenyan boy, now a successful carpenter.**

When the North thinks of the South, it is often an image of hopelessness: drought and destruction, floods and debt. Weeping fathers and mothers in disaster-ridden countries burying their children wrapped in old rags. Malnourished children with distended bellies, noses streaming with mucus, and faces covered with flies. Once proud and dignified men, women, and children begging for food with cupped hands — these are all common images in television and newspaper articles.

However, in the North and the South, the causes of poverty which make people vulnerable to disasters receive scant attention.

Despite some decades of "development", most of the Southern nations are in desperate shape. Having pursued economic strategies largely modelled on Northern experience and inappropriate to local conditions, the countries find themselves deeply in debt and unable to extricate themselves from the quagmire of poverty.

The poor, who have been seldom more than mute actors in plays conjured up in the capital cities of the North and the South, have become further alienated in their own societies. Poverty continues to spread its tentacles further and further.

It is easy to lament over the plight of the poor. A UN information leaflet entitled "When food is hope", published recently, describes the situation in this way: "For tens of millions of hungry people in the developing world, life is little more than prolonged agony, a futile battle against despair."

But for the poor, despair is a luxury which they can ill-afford. And throughout the South, there are seeds of hope. These are sown by citizens' groups.

Against all the odds, tenacious people have started small projects — even some big ones. Out of the bankruptcy and poverty of failed international and national development strategies, a new set of organisations have emerged among the poor.

Change and development are taking place at local levels. Individuals, families, and communities are planning, organising to survive in difficult environments. Tens of thousands of such groups have been identified across Asia, Africa and Latin America. In scores of countries, women's groups, peasant groups, religious organisations, consumer campaigners, and environment protection societies, are acting as important engines of change.

This book tries to capture the spirit behind nine such projects, in Bangladesh, India, Indonesia, Kenya, Sri Lanka, Tanzania and Zambia. It deals with ordinary people and how they have broken through the poverty trap:

- In India, women pavement dwellers in Bombay, often described as the "wretched of the city", have through the Society for Promotion of Area Resource Centres (SPARC) designed and built their own low-cost houses. And Mahiti has helped women in a remote salt-ridden village in Gujarat to develop their community and stop migration to the city.

INTRODUCTION

- In Tanzania, the Community Development Trust Fund (CDTF) has helped an impoverished village to set up a village clinic, which has transformed people's health.
- In Bangladesh, Proshika assists landless peasants to set up an irrigation scheme to benefit poor farmers.
- In Kenya, Undugu is assisting Nairobi's "parking boys" to develop a better future for themselves. And self-help schemes established by the Kenyan Water for Health Organisation (KWAHO) provide safe drinking water and have improved sanitation in villages.
- In Sri Lanka, a group of formerly unemployed youths are helping Nation Builders to re-forest denuded lands, using indigenous tree species.
- In Indonesia, Dian Desa has enabled people to free themselves from the daily trudge to a mountain stream for water: four kilometres uphill, and then back again.
- In Zambia, marginal farmers in a drought prone area have worked with the Village Development Foundation (VDF) to boost agricultural production.

These nine projects were selected with the help of the authors on the cover of this book: three women and five men. All of them are journalists, and nationals of countries where the projects are located. All the photographs have also been taken by Southern photographers.

After selecting the projects, Panos asked each journalist to write a 5,000-word report. "We want your story, not propaganda pieces for the organisation," they were told. The authors were asked some specific questions: Who evolved the projects? Do the people really benefit? Are the schemes sustainable?

Panos also asked the journalists to visit the project sites, to speak to the project officials, go through evaluation reports, and above all, to listen to the people whom the projects are intended to benefit.

For Southern journalists, gathering information on development projects can be a tricky business, particularly when government departments, aid agencies, or multilateral organisations are involved. The relatively easy task of getting one's hands on a crucial report or fixing an interview with an official can be a nightmare of delays and bureaucratic red tape.

But the workers in the non-governmental organisations (NGOs) responsible for the schemes were open and honest about their experiences. Despite skeleton staffs and meagre budgets, many found time to brief the journalists and accompany them to the project sites. As reported in the book, some were even critical of their own efforts.

There can never be a final word on how to improve the lives of the poor. This book is intended as contribution to a discussion on development that should provide not only material gains, but also help people take control of their lives.

The reports present the situation in each project as the journalists have found them. They are not the views of Panos. They vividly describe the way that people have found solutions to seemingly irredeemable problems. Their experiences are relevant to people in other parts of the world as well.

The reports also contain tough and critical observations. As one author wrote: "Being a cynical journalist, I see many more years of struggle ahead."

Against All Odds is the third in a series of Panos books written by Southern journalists. The first, *Towards Sustainable Development,* evaluates 14 development projects funded by Nordic donors. The second, *War Wounds*, paints a graphic description of the impact of civil war on development through the eyes of Sudanese writers.

Most evaluations of projects carried out by non-governmental organisations (NGOs) are written by foreign experts or officials from the organisations themselves. This book is unique: for the first time, a collection of independent reports on NGO projects in the South has been written by Southern journalists.

Donatus de Silva
Director, Regional Programmes
The Panos Institute

CONTENTS

INDIA: The pavement dwellers of Bombay	2
TANZANIA: A life-saving clinic in remote Chanika	28
BANGLADESH: Breaking the grip of greedy landowners	44
KENYA: The parking boys of Nairobi	64
INDIA: No longer need they abandon home	88
KENYA: The water that brings new life	112
SRI LANKA: Growing trees in the light of the Buddha	132
ZAMBIA: The same hands, but new minds	150
INDONESIA: Ending the daily water chore	168

INDIA

THE PAVEMENT DWELLERS OF BOMBAY

DARRYL D'MONTE

INDIA: The pavement dwellers of Bombay

DARRYL D'MONTE

"Would you even spit here?" Triveni asks in disgust. She lives in a covered cot on one of the pavements of Kamathipura, the red-light district in central Bombay. She gestures to the narrow space between her abode and the next cot, which is occupied by a man. Both covered beds jut out at right angles to the street.

"I have to do everything here," Triveni continues angrily. "I cook here and at the crack of dawn I bathe here in full view of everybody. And when the rains come, the water collects and rises right up to our cots. What are we supposed to do?"

Triveni is one of the people who are known in India as "pavement dwellers". They are truly "the wretched of the city", existing a notch lower down the social scale than even the despised slum dwellers. The people of the pavements evoke intense feelings among Bombay's better-off citizens — revulsion, hostility, sometimes pity.

India's Supreme Court, which for four years from 1981 deliberated on the legal status of these hapless residents and finally ruled against them, gave this Dickensian description of their existence: "They cook and sleep where they please, for no conveniences are available to them. Their daughters, come of age, bathe under the nosy gaze of passers-by, unmindful of the feminine sense of bashfulness.

"The cooking and washing over, women pick lice from each

INDIA: The pavement dwellers of Bombay

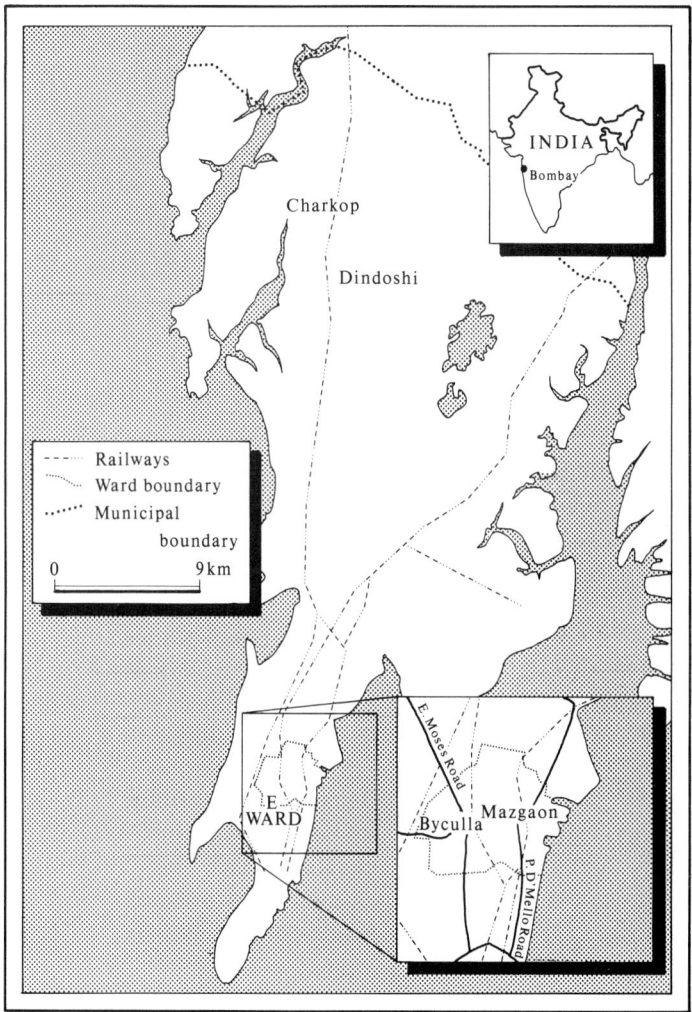

Bombay

other's hair. The boys beg. Menfolk without occupation snatch neck-chains with the connivance of the defenders of law and order. When caught, if at all, they say: 'Who doesn't commit crimes in the city'?"

If the Supreme Court, generally regarded as a liberal institution and upholder of many democratic rights, gives this graphic portrayal, one can imagine the attitude of less tolerant sections of Indian society.

The very fact that no one has yet counted the exact number of pavement dwellers in Bombay, the country's commercial and industrial capital, or in India's other cities for that matter, speaks eloquently of society's indifference.

The findings of the latest national census in 1981 have not yet been disclosed, but the proportion of pavement to slum dwellers in 1971 was officially put at less than one to a hundred. In Bombay, that would mean about 50,000 pavement dwellers among the estimated 5.5 million slum dwellers who form half the city's population.

Unofficially, however, the All-India Slum Dwellers' Welfare Association — a loose network of NGOs, estimates that 100,000 people are living on Bombay's pavements, and six times as many on the sidewalks of Calcutta.

Nauseating eyesore

Unlike slums, which however derelict they may be, have the potential to be "regularised" and "improved" by the authorities, pavement dwellings are simply regarded as a nauseating eyesore and nuisance to pedestrians.

The pavement dwellers, the poorest of the poor, are the most recent migrants from India's rural areas to cities such as Bombay. Typically, they have been pushed off their plots because of environmental degradation; drought makes it impossible for them to eke out an existence on their land, or to find work on the holdings of others.

Their only alternative to starvation is to trek to the cities, pitch a tent of rags on the most convenient pavement they can find, and then look for ways to earn something to eat.

Most of the pavement dwellers live along or near the railway tracks, because from there it is easier to travel in search of work and to sell vegetables and fruit to middle-class commuters on their way home from office jobs.

Bombay's slum dwellers are not well organised because they are

INDIA: The pavement dwellers of Bombay

'They cook and sleep where they please, for no conveniences are available to them. Their daughters, come of age, bathe under the nosy gaze of passers-by ...' — *Indian Supreme Court*

scattered throughout the length and breadth of the metropolis and have no regular work. The pavement dwellers have still less status and are not even mentioned as a category in any mobilisation programme.

Observes A. Jockin, secretary of the National Slum Dwellers' Federation: "Although some organisations deal with both slum and pavement dwellers, the latter can hardly be said to be active as a group."

Although Bombay's pavement dwellers form part of the mosaic of "ecological refugees" migrating to cities and towns all over India, no other city has as large a proportion of pavement and slum dwellers to total population. The reason is that many jobs are available in the informal sector, as a back-up to the large-scale employment possibilities in factories and offices. Moreover, Bombay and the not-too-distant city of Pune account for more than six out of every ten industrial jobs in Maharashtra state, which is notoriously drought-prone.

In 1983, India's Planning Commission reported that Maharashtra had the highest slum population in the country — 6.62 million or nearly a third of its urban population. The state had nearly 20% of all the slum dwellers in India.

Laying down the law

It was, in fact, because of the Maharashtra government's attempts to carry out mass evictions of pavement dwellers in 1981 that Indian law on the subject became established.

Two activist groups in Bombay — the Lawyers' Collective and the People's Union of Civil Liberties — obtained a stay on these evictions in the city High Court. The case went to the Supreme Court in Delhi, which finally ruled in 1985 that people had no fundamental right to set up homes on the roadside. However, they could only be evicted on certain conditions, such as being given advance notice and, in some cases, alternative sites to live on.

The 1985 judgment is the foundation of official policy regarding the legality of pavement dwellings. But the World Bank has meanwhile been assisting the housing authorities in several Indian

INDIA: The pavement dwellers of Bombay

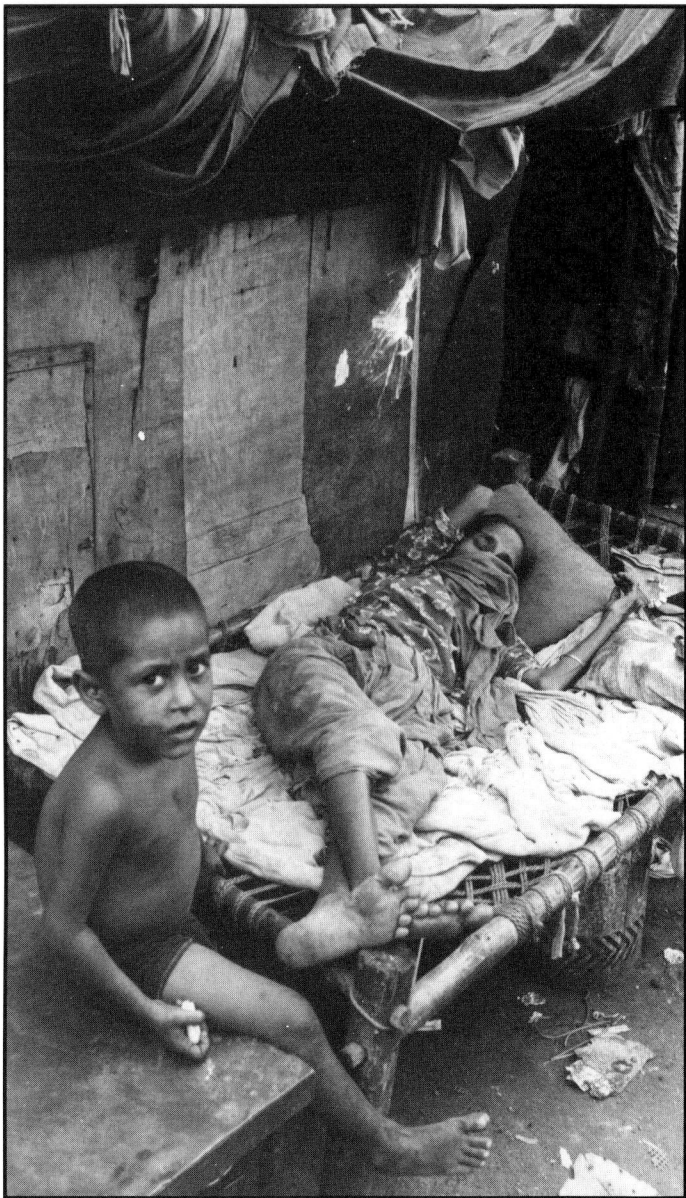

Bombay's pavement dwellers: a notch further down the social scale than even the despised slum dwellers.

cities, notably Madras, to prepare site and service schemes — serviced plots of land for self-building — and with slum improvement in general.

Under the Bank's influence, India's bureaucrats are slowly coming round to the view that it is futile to try to remove slum and pavement dwellers and that it is a much better line of action to improve their homes, either where they already exist or on a vacant site.

But this attitude began to be formed only after the people had undergone much despair and insecurity: researchers at Bombay's College of Social Work have found that the average slum dweller has been forced to move home, because of official demolition programmes, no less than five times.

Start of SPARC

An NGO in Bombay called the Society for Promotion of Area Resource Centres, known by its less ungainly acronym, SPARC, has meanwhile been mobilising the pavement families to change things so as to better themselves.

The director, Sheela Patel, and her colleagues registered SPARC in 1984 under the Societies Registration Act. Patel recalls that "there were certain strata which no organisation was reaching. These were the people living on the brink of illegality — it required an altogether new set-up to deal with them. But we did have the advantage of knowing the area very well."

> *'These were the people living on the brink of illegality — it required an altogether new set-up to deal with them.'*

Patel had previously worked for several years as the assistant director of Nagpada Neighbourhood House, a conventional social-service organisation in the same area of Bombay – E Ward.

SPARC members are quite open about the fact that, at the outset, their organisation consisted completely of middle-class professionals who wanted to break new ground. There was not a single pavement dweller in their ranks. The founder members had experience in fields as diverse as counselling, community health, child welfare, community organisation, social science research and biomedical sciences. They had, however, come to realise that poor people could be the object of research without understanding its true purpose or implications, and that such people could simply be used to further the careers of those who came around asking questions.

"We knew what we didn't want to do, what tradition we didn't want to follow," says Mona Daswani. "But we had no idea at the beginning what sort of issue we should take up."

Yet a feature of SPARC which emerged later as its unique strength, and which enabled it to intervene with confidence in the world of Bombay's pavement dwellers, was one of the area's existing resources: the women who bore the brunt of homelessness, firstly as rural migrants and then as females and who had to suffer their lot silently for cultural reasons.

It was the suffering and stoic silence of these women that made them, in SPARC's telling phrase, the "invisible contributors" to the organisation's effectiveness.

As Sheela Patel and Srilatha Batliwala, another SPARC founder-member, acknowledge: "We were a group interested in the problems of pavement people, but we didn't know what to do and we had nothing material to give. We wanted to sit and talk with the women and see if we could understand their problems and work with them to find solutions."

Band-aid schemes

Adds Mona Daswani: "The welfare approach amounts to no more than band-aid schemes providing short-term alleviation. It can actually increase the dependency of the poor whereas non-formal education is a more permanent asset that can always stand them in good stead. The question we asked ourselves was: Can we focus on bringing information to the people and thereby bring them together as a community?"

It was after the Supreme Court judgment in what came to be known as "the pavement dwellers' case" that SPARC activists made their first move into housing. They decided that an effective way to counter and head off the threat of eviction of the residents with whom they were dealing was simply to count them to see what strength they had in numbers.

SPARC's area of operation in E Ward, comprising roughly the precincts of Byculla and Mazgaon, is one of the most crowded and poorest parts of Bombay.

The organisation conducted a census in 1985 of about 6,000 households living on the pavements in this ward and the converging arterial roads, and found that more than 25% earned between only Rs7 – Rs12 (US$0.50 to $0.86) a day. A similar number earned less than Rs6 (US$0.43) a day. Nearly half the households were Muslim.

While most of the residents were unskilled labourers, and some of them petty vendors of vegetables and other necessities, almost all the women worked as domestic helps in nearby middle-class homes.

The possibility of finding employment is an important element in SPARC's ongoing "training" programmes to empower women to improve their lot. Any distant resettlement site is therefore ruled out because it is less likely to have sources of income nearby.

A participatory exercise

The census proved a participatory exercise, with the women who were being interviewed about the details of their households then turning round and cross-examining the investigators. Indeed, any outsider who interacts with women trained by SPARC comes away quite sobered by the boldness with which his or her own assumptions are queried.

The census had the effect of mobilising the women, of giving them a feeling that they weren't alone but shared an identity with many others.

Patel and Batliwala express it thus: "Without exception, the item of data which stirred everyone was the large number of people surveyed. The fact that in just one segment of the city there were 27,000 others like themselves moved and visibly strengthened the pavement dwellers. "Their feeling was: 'There are so many of us! Thousands and thousands! They can't just sweep us away like dust'."

Women in the census area said that the Supreme Court judgment had forced them to think about their future on the pavements. It reminded them that they had never intended to live on pavements permanently, where their children after them would have to face the same trials and humiliations.

Demolitions heighten insecurity

Late in 1985, there were threats of demolitions of pavement dwellings. In March 1986, some 300 families living in E Moses Road in the same vicinity were forcibly moved to Dindoshi in the northern suburb of Goregaon, where the municipal corporation provided plots measuring 3 x 5 metres (10 x 15 feet). Soon afterwards, another 1,500 families were moved from a different part of the city to Dindoshi, heightening the insecurity of all the pavement dwellers.

'Do you think we enjoy living on the pavement? If they gave us proper houses we'd live as decently as they do.'

There were no large-scale evictions in Bombay during 1987, however, probably because of sensitivity that it was International Year of Shelter for the Homeless (IYSH). Nevertheless, civil liberties groups feared that there might again be mass demolitions of the flimsy dwellings in the months to come.

"All they want to do is get rid of us," many of the women complained bitterly. "But if they do, who will sweep and swab their floors and wash their dirty dishes and clothes for such a pittance? Do you think we enjoy living on the pavement? If they gave us proper houses we'd live as decently as they do."

SPARC realised that the contribution the pavement dwellers made to the urban economy went unrecognised. In fact, the number of persons in any slum or pavement household who go out and work is much higher than in the average Indian family.

Moreover, they contribute to the city's coffers by paying indirect taxes such as "octroi", a levy on all commodities coming into the city, including edibles. The allegation that they are scavengers is therefore off the mark.

Becoming defiant

Threats of overnight eviction triggered off many meetings where, in an atmosphere of great tension, women discussed what they should do. When a woman at one meeting said: "If they break our shelters, we'll have to go back to the village", the others pounced on her. "Go back to what?" they demanded rhetorically. "To starve like we did before? We can never go back — no matter what they do to us."

Meek submission before the might of the authorities was clearly giving way to defiance. Still, no one knew what the next step should be. But the expected mass evictions of slum and pavement dwellers did not take place and this gave the women of E Ward a little breathing space to plan a strategy.

Word had reached E Ward that Dindoshi, 40 kilometres (25 miles) away, was an idyllic site, with plenty of fresh air and hills nearby, "like it used to be in the village". So SPARC decided as its next move to organise a trip to Dindoshi to check it out as a place that could sustain a poor community.

The reality of that resettlement proved to be quite different from the rumours. It shattered the brief euphoria. The pavement women who accompanied the SPARC members spread out in small groups and talked freely with the resettled families. By the time they returned home their sense of envy and hope had been replaced by fear and depression.

They had seen the harsh, barren landscape without a single tree for shelter from the sun. The "large" plots were strewn with enormous boulders which not only reduced the space available, but were also encumbrances, which made movement and communication with neighbours difficult.

Nor had the settlers been given the necessary materials to build adequate dwellings. And not only had most of the women involved

SPARC activists and pavement dwellers discuss the pros and cons of housing projects.

lost the jobs they'd had before, but their isolated location now made it impossible to find employment nearby.

Dindoshi is a good example of how *not* to go about "resettling" families, according to SPARC personnel.

Empowering women to act for themselves

The Dindoshi experience confirmed the activists in their belief that, only when the pavement women understood all the aspects of their housing problem, and not simply how to get a roof over their heads, would they truly be empowered to deal with their situation with any hope of success.

It was a question of furnishing them with all the relevant information and enabling them to perceive the economic and social contexts within which any community has to live.

But why zero in on the *women*? Why not focus on the menfolk who, in India's male-chauvinist society, are at least accorded a modicum of respect because of their gender ? Why waste one's energy on the weakest of the weak when it is strength that is needed to change the situation?

This is a question which many workers on other housing projects have asked SPARC since it was established. And SPARC's answer has always been that it believes in working with women both as a philosophy and for reasons of strategy.

Women have been excluded from making decisions about housing although they bear the brunt of all the problems which arise from the lack of shelter. And in many of the poorest abodes, it is actually the women who are the breadwinners.

It is the women who have to turn a shelter into a home, SPARC workers argue persuasively, and who must in the first place set up all the family's survival systems — the water source, the cooking fuel, the health care, and the education of the children.

It is the women who suffer most from the lack of proper latrines and bathing areas. It is they who are blamed when a child dashes from the pavement shelter and is hit by a truck passing close by. And it is they themselves who are to blame, according to the malevolent male logic prevalent throughout the world, if they or their daughters are raped when they go outside in the darkness to relieve themselves.

It is the women who must bear the wrath of the demolition squads who arrive when their husbands are away at work; and who, when the destruction has taken place and the children are exposed to the elements, tie their saris to bamboo poles to shelter their loved ones from the sun.

SPARC workers believe it is clear as crystal that no one is more committed to changing the conditions of the pavement people than the women who head those wretched families.

Crucial lack of knowledge

A major cause of the failure of previous attempts by pavement dwellers to win adequate resettlement from the authorities was the lack of knowledge about the city's land policy and housing schemes. Moreover, various intermediaries — whether their own local leaders, politicians and even activist groups and voluntary agencies — had negotiated on their behalf and made decisions which affected their lives centrally while they were left to stand on the sidelines.

This is what made SPARC look for a method which would enable women pavement dwellers to view alternatives themselves, at first hand, and allow them to come up with something more useful than a mere replication of present housing on another site.

Submission before the might of the authorities is giving way to defiance.

Such knowledge, SPARC believed, would eventually give women the confidence to take control of their lives. The knowledge would enable them to do critiques of the expensive "low-cost" designs churned out by architects and town planners who were out of touch with pavement reality. And in the process, women would learn something about methods of financing and land-tenure arrangements.

Unless an approach of this kind was adopted, "resettlement", such as the scandalous shambles at Dindoshi, would be repeated ad nauseam and keep resulting in nothing better than "government-initiated slums".

Unless people came to understand the means whereby they were being peripheralised, they would not be able to change the situation, SPARC believed. In Dindoshi, as in other resettlement projects aided by the World Bank, many of those who were allotted sites sold out and returned to their miserable existence in the city centre due to the inescapable pressure of market forces.

People, no matter how poor they are, simply have to live within reach of jobs, within reach of safe drinking water, and within the hope of being able eventually to improve their condition. That is the principal reason why, according to SPARC, they should enter the decision-making process through collective action.

Patel and her co-workers were convinced that the women were in no way stupid just because they were illiterate. They had gained their experience of life literally on the streets, and there was no textbook that could compete with their understanding of what they needed. Their understanding could be honed and made useful in an institutional setting through a process of awareness-training.

"We did not restrict ourselves to any particular project," SPARC observes in one of its own documents. "Rather, we were and always are ready to train any number of women who are keen to learn. Not only does the training make the women into a valuable community resource, it enables them in their turn to become effective trainers of other women. At that point our own role is reduced to one of support."

Putting theory into practice

It was according to this strategy that SPARC arranged for groups of pavement women to visit vacant sites in mid-town Bombay that were not very far from E Ward. Any two of the five sites inspected would be large enough to house all the pavement dwellers of Bombay.

The next step would be for women to conduct their own census to determine the number of families eligible for relocation. Thirdly, groups of women would take over various administrative functions of implementing decisions taken by the community — become, in fact, "managers". Finally, and most ambitious, there would be a workshop on housing design and construction, culminating in an exhibition of the models created by the women themselves.

To implement the strategy, SPARC's training process consisted of groups of 20 women going to view vacant sites in an informal way, combining the recreational atmosphere of a picnic with the serious talk of noting and listing the pros and cons of particular locations.

> *'The complex nature of urban planning was what the women became immersed in and began to grasp.'*

As Jockin notes: "The complex nature of urban planning was what the women became immersed in and began to grasp. For example, how much time and money would be spent on transport to the new site, what markets are there nearby, what water supplies, what health facilities and other services."

The next stage — a census by the women revealed interesting dynamics of life on the pavement. But it also highlighted an important principle: the constant desire of SPARC activists themselves to learn as they go along.

This has the salutary effect of breathing an air of democratic participation, a sense that everyone is complementary to everyone else, into every activity which the organisation undertakes, whether it is research or practical action.

For the census, about 40 "clusters" were identified in E Ward. A cluster was defined as a group of pavement dwellings which could include anything between 25 and 250 hutments and of up to 2,500 people.

Re-thinking basic concepts

The very concept of what constitutes a family had to be rethought, with varying numbers of people living in abodes of different physical sizes at different times of the day and night, and other permutations not common in middle-class housing.

For instance, would a daughter, abandoned by her husband and living with three children in her father's hut, be entitled to housing, or would she be considered a dependant of her father? People had to think through all these issues, using the unhappy experiences of the families at Dindoshi to guide them.

The women's census proceeded without any major hitch. But as it set about organising groups to consider aspects of housing design in different clusters of E Ward, SPARC began to encounter criticism. This came from people who believed that it was no use focusing on the rehousing of only one section of the community, but that the entire housing problem had to be tackled.

Members of the groups included former prostitutes, for example Triveni in Kamathipura, who still works as a collector of cash for a brothel-keeper handling hundreds of rupees a night. She was included because she has natural leadership qualities. But some independent observers of SPARC's activities believe it was a good example of how the empowerment exercise was being overdone: they thought that the process of selecting the groups was too arbitrary.

The women's own house designs

In discussing the third and fourth stages, a SPARC worker says: "When we first suggested that women could design their own homes, we were met with disbelief, even a sense of awe. However, it soon dawned on the women that a home was more than just four walls and that it was they, the women, who were responsible for the efficient use of internal space."

An alternative housing project in Bombay, partly government-funded, inspected by women pavement dwellers.

The workshop consisted of getting the women systematically to think, on the basis of their everyday experience, about the kind of dwelling that would best suit their situation. And they were encouraged to think of designing the dwellings on the modular principle, that is, in a way which would allow extra sections to be added later when more money becomes available, such as a loft for storage, or a porch.

The women also had to become familiar with a process that turned out to be quite complicated for them — costing the shelters they designed, including the price of labour.

The six-month workshop culminated in March 1987, with an

exhibition in the area immediately adjacent to the SPARC office, which is housed in a decrepit municipal clinic in Byculla, a suburb of Bombay. Four types of home were demonstrated with full-size models made of tin sheets and sacking. Each model had been meticulously costed and ranged from Rs5,900 (US$422) to Rs13,000 (US$930). SPARC considers that the housing design workshop has been its most notable achievement.

> *'The demonstration attracted official attention and was visited by Bombay's top officials.'*

The demonstration attracted official attention and was visited by Bombay's top officials, including P.S.A. Sundaram, chief administrator of the Maharashtra Housing and Development Authority, and V.K. Date, director of the World Bank slum improvement scheme. Both men were impressed by the affirmation, in such a practical way, that a woman is indeed "the architect of the home".

Date promised to offer some land where these enterprising women could implement their housing skills. A number of plots measuring 18 square metres (200 square feet) have since been allotted to house 300 families in the distant suburb of Charkop.

SPARC has, however, been hesitating to move any families from E Ward, because by moving they would lose their jobs and sink even further into poverty. Instead, it has been encouraging women to save Rs50 (US$3.50) a month in bank accounts towards a housing fund which they operate themselves.

But the delay in moving is wearing the women's patience thin. Snaps Triveni as she perches on her cot on the pavement: "Four months ago we put numbers up on our homes to identify the families who were to move. A whole year has been wasted in these interminable meetings. They tell you to get ready and then there's some delay or other — one time it's the engineers, then it's someone else. If we have been made accountable, why can't SPARC hold the engineers responsible too?"

Jockin, who has worked with SPARC since 1985 while

continuing to run the National Slum Dwellers' Federation, is trying to convince the authorities to allocate plots to the E Ward women which are closer to their present homes in exchange for the land in Charkop.

Affecting the environment

SPARC's work in the domain of resettlement and housing has a tremendous bearing on Bombay's environment. It has been demonstrating that pavement and slum dwellers need not be, in the words of the Supreme Court judgment, consigned to living "in the midst of filth with rabid dogs in search of stinking meat and cats in search of hungry rats to keep them company ... "

As the organisation's name makes clear, its work is all about better utilisation of scarce resources — land itself, building materials and people's skills.

> *'We didn't have the courage to speak up; now we can stand up to them. We didn't know what a "mahila milan" (women's meeting) was; now we save money. We do everything.'*

For one thing, locating pavement dwellers nearer their work places will have important implications for the city's overburdened train and bus services. The provision of sanitation and drainage at resettlement sites will also improve health conditions, since most of the diseases which afflict the people are water-borne.

But has SPARC been successful? There are contradictory views about this. The subtlety of the issues involved do not permit a cut-and-dried answer: the work being done in E Ward is a matter of emphasis and style.

While Triveni, who is herself a leader of people, appears to be sceptical, others on her street are more favourable in their assessment. Sona, also a former prostitute, says: "We didn't have the courage to speak up; now we can stand up to them. We didn't know what a 'mahila milan' (women's meeting) was; now we save money. We do everything. Our lives have been spent on these pavements; our children at least should have a brighter future."

Although it is a conspicuous fact that SPARC has no concrete achievement to its credit, that it has not yet been able to resettle a single pavement dweller, Mona Daswani argues that it is not by physical indices alone that SPARC's contribution should be measured. The organisation's effectiveness has rather to do with what Batliwala terms "the quality of communication — the ability to mobilise large groups of people" who previously had simply been abandoned to their fate.

She recognises in particular the experience which Jockin, a grassroots worker involved in resistance to demolitions for over a decade, has brought to the middle-class professionals: "The unproductive clash of two different consciousnesses — that of activists and intellectuals — has been eliminated."

The overwhelming achievement of SPARC has been the psychological empowerment of women. So much so that the outcome of the training in the social and economic aspects of housing was as much an eye-opener for its members as it was for the pavement-dwelling women.

"As the women became more confident," SPARC reports, "they took over the training and taught us more about group dynamics and processes than we would ever find in anyone's theory. The women made demands on us, and in the process they taught us how to train them."

Anyone who visits the SPARC office and attends a "mahila milan" meeting where someone is being screened for a loan, or a housing meeting in Dindoshi, cannot but be moved by the confidence with which the poorest of the poor now conduct themselves. It is a strong antidote to the popular belief that Indian women in general, and the poor in particular, are spineless and submissive.

The reservations of critics

Nevertheless, Anand Grover of the Lawyers' Collective believes that E Ward women have become dependent on the activists, rather than self-reliant. "They turn to Sheela Patel for everything," he remarks. "All the time it's ask 'didi' (sister) this, ask 'didi' that."

Grover compares the way SPARC works with the methods of the Jhopadpatti Rahavasi Sangh (Hutment Dwellers' Federation) on P.D'Mello Road, which runs from the city centre, where pavement dwellers have organised themselves to fight demolitions and are, it would seem, more "militant". The Lawyers' Collective has played, according to him, a behind-the-scenes role as professional advisors to the Sangh.

Another activist, who does not wish to be identified adds: "SPARC is more social-work oriented. There is no organising done in terms of struggle. Its approach is somewhat studentish. When there was a 'morcha' (marching) demonstration of 5,000 people on P. D'Mello Road, we saw a SPARC activist moving about with a video camera, recording the scene. Their meetings have a clubbish atmosphere, with tea and lunch served to everybody."

The traditional militant approach of mobilisation and struggle, with — needless to say — men in the forefront, contrasts sharply with the slower, more democratic and, it can be argued, ultimately more meaningful efforts of SPARC.

A different atmosphere

Nevertheless, within the clusters with which it has interacted since 1984, SPARC certainly enjoys tremendous popularity, as can easily be witnessed at its meetings and other activities. Precisely because it is a group of women, there is an altogether different intimacy: much affection, badinage, abuse and anger, often at the same time. It is difficult to imagine such camaraderie — middle-class professionals mingling unselfconsciously with the lowest rungs of society — in other activist groups of any kind in India.

SPARC has deliberately chosen not to become too institutionalised, which is why it does not even possess a proper office, though it has 20 full-time workers, 10 co-ordinators and another 10 part-time workers. Meetings are conducted with everyone squatting on mats on the floor of the converted garage in the same compound as the office. Activists and pavement women often share a meal.

INDIA: The pavement dwellers of Bombay

SPARC more than justifies itself by enabling poor women on the streets to make their voices heard for the first time.

As for funding, the organisation has hitherto sought the bulk from the government for its research and training activities — including an ambitious country-wide study of drug addiction, undertaken because it has come to realise how vulnerable the urban poor are to the menace of narcotics. Even if the government funds, which come from different ministries, were to be withdrawn, the organisation feels it can fall back on international donors. But it would only do so, it says, if absolutely necessary.

The pros and cons

One concludes, therefore, with a résumé of SPARC's pros and cons

- The organisation makes too much of a fetish about "deprofessionalising" skills. As the Delhi-based architect S.K. Das points out: "Our societal responsibility as professionals is to influence the women as much as be influenced by them, even while the final decision rests with them."

- SPARC is also somewhat weak ideologically. It does not seem to be clear about who should play what role, and leaves too much to happenstance.

- Nevertheless, SPARC has filled a genuine gap. It is probably in reaction to the conventional militancy of activist slum groups that it has emerged as an alternative in its own right, which does not pretend to know all the answers to housing the homeless and then impose its solutions on the poor.
- The most fundamental reality is that SPARC is operating in an extremely male-dominated and hierarchical society. Even if it fails to achieve very much in physical terms, even if it does not throw in its lot with broad struggles for housing rights, it more than justifies itself by enabling poor women on the streets to make their voices heard for the first time.

TANZANIA

A LIFE-SAVING CLINIC IN REMOTE CHANIKA

ANTHONY NGAIZA

TANZANIA:
A life-saving clinic in remote Chanika

ANTHONY NGAIZA

For most of its history the impoverished farming community of Chanika was just another dusty, insignificant and inaccessible village 30 kilometres (18 miles) southwest of Tanzania's capital, Dar es Salaam.

The 750 villagers in this isolated rural community, which depends on the peasant cultivation of rice and maize, hardly knew what a malaria tablet or a qualified medical doctor looked like. "Medication," recalls a village official, "was prescribed by medicine-men".

Chanika was no different from the villages in most other countries in the South where the rural population keeps the wheels of development turning by growing food and providing raw materials for industry.

But for Chanika, as with elsewhere, all the basic amenities like hospitals and health facilities were centred in the towns. And the lack of transport and communications made it impossible for the villagers to go there in search of medical care.

Yet now, any casual visitor to the village will notice two remarkable features — a crowd of baby-hugging and expectant mothers bustling around a medical clinic, and the surprisingly good health of the population. For good health is rare even in urban areas which have most of the medical personnel and facilities.

At Chanika there is hope and confidence. Very few people are

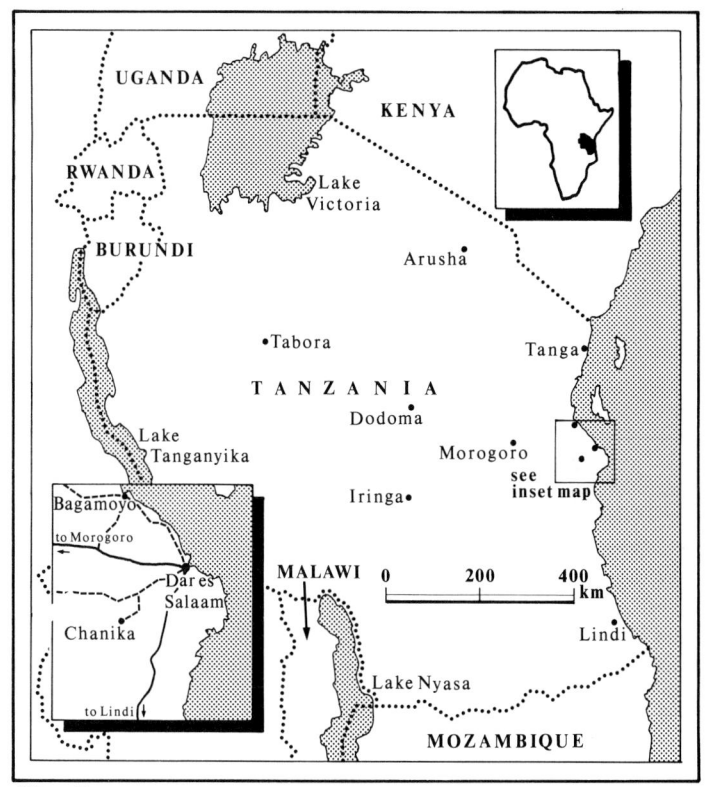

TANZANIA: A life-saving clinic in remote Chanika

Chanika

dying from infections such as malaria, the biggest killer disease in Africa. And, with some government help, the villagers have also managed to carve out a 10-kilometre feeder road connecting Chanika with the main road to the nearest town, Kisarawe.

This is in sharp contrast with earlier years when the village suffered a heavy toll of death. "Not a single week passed without someone passing away. Our eyes were used to seeing corpses, our hands to digging graves and our hearts to endless frustration," laments Idris Shabaan, a member of the village Defence Committee who lost two close relatives in 1974.

The foundation for the dramatic change was laid in 1975 when thousands of unemployed from Dar es Salaam came and settled in

Chanika in response to the government's "back-to-the-land" campaign.

The newcomers lead to change

At first, Chanika became a flashpoint as the new settlers challenged the shaky village establishment and existing social order. The police and the people's militia had to be called to keep the peace.

But after several tense months the newcomers came to accept their resettlement. They were smoothly integrated into the social and economic fabric of the village and Chanika became their beacon of hope. "We accomplished this through persuasion and political education, not coercion," explains Mustapha Songambele, the now-retired Coast Region Commissioner who directed the resettlement campaign. "We made sacrifices and now Chanika is the pride of the region."

> *'Not a single week passed without someone passing away. Our eyes were used to seeing corpses, our hands to digging graves and our hearts to endless frustration.'*

This is no idle boast. By all accounts Chanika is a success story; the invasion of the settlers caused a population explosion that made it necessary to introduce important public amenities, including educational and health facilities, that the village did not have before. It was the settlers who made the central government in Dar es Salaam realise that Chanika existed.

The story of Chanika's development begins in 1976 with the construction of a health clinic which the villagers still see as their living monument. Its construction was very dramatic.

The villagers held a "baraza" (meeting) at which they decided that they needed a clinic and dispensary to deal with their health problems. In their search for funds to build the clinic, they first sent a delegation to the district headquarters in Kisarawe to ask for a loan.

The district did not have the resources to help them directly but

TANZANIA: A life-saving clinic in remote Chanika

Chanika village: lack of transport made it impossible for villagers to travel to town to obtain medical assistance.

officials realised that the situation was serious and passed on the request to the Community Development Trust Fund (CDTF) of Tanzania.

Funding people projects

CDTF is a non-governmental, non-profit making charitable trust founded in Dar es Salaam in 1962. It provides funds only to those projects which are initiated and carried out by the people themselves.

Its sources of funding, which have varied over the years, have included some 40 donor agencies and charities in Europe, the United States, Canada and New Zealand — more than 99% of them non-governmental.

Chanika's application to CDTF succeeded as it clearly met the minimum requirements for a loan. Eight months later the villagers

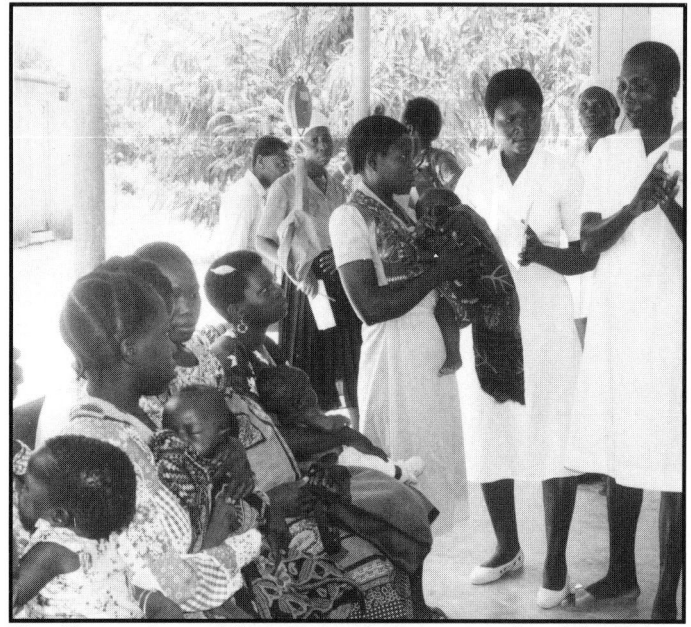

The villagers also contributed towards the construction of the clinic.

began to build their clinic. The fund contributed US$1,500 towards the total cost of about US$5,000.

The clinic was finished within a year during which the villagers made whatever contributions they could to its construction. "We see this clinic as our pride and the biggest achievement in the village's living memory," says Said Geshi, Chanika's elder and leader. "It is a project of self-reliance."

Willing Villagers

Chanika ward councillor Miraji Ally describes how the villagers volunteered to make bricks, draw water, fetch sand and work as unpaid labourers. "Perhaps they wanted to show that the government was incapable of governing," he jokes.

He was surprised at the villagers' attitude. "The 'back-to-the-land' campaigns certainly produced some impressive results countrywide," he says, "but nowhere else can you find the kind of miracle performed by the Chanika villagers".

Once the clinic was built the government provided the doctors and nurses to staff it. They are paid by the district authorities with funds provided mainly by various Nordic countries.

Before the clinic was built, officials estimate that 10% of pregnant women died before and during childbirth and more than 20% of the children died before they were six months old.

The villagers had turned to some bogus medicine-men, as a last resort. "Whenever people died, we rushed to them and they told us we had been bewitched or fallen victim to evil spirits," says one elderly woman.

But the villagers paid heavily for the advice from the local medicine-men which rarely relieved suffering and frequently made matters worse. "People found out too late that it was disastrous to go to bogus medicine-men," says the doctor in charge of the clinic, Ndele Mmboma. "They regretted it when they had to pay too high a price."

The clinic saves lives

The clinic has changed all this. According to health officials, more than 85% of the villagers now depend on it. "Only 15% are still locked in superstition but we are fighting to bring them round," Dr Mmboma explains.

"We see this project as our life blood," says Mrs Maua Said, who had just taken her three-month-old baby for treatment. Mrs Fatima Ismail, a mother of four in her sixth month of pregnancy, says her experiences with her first three children, born before the clinic was built, were "terrible".

'We see this project as our life blood.'

The women believe that the clinic has saved many lives. There used to be almost daily deaths from childbirth but now safe deliveries are the rule rather than the exception. Mrs Mkejina Abdala has one child, Wema Kondo, but she says she would like to have "more and more children now that the clinic is here".

There is one area, however, where conservative traditions and cultural taboos have prevented much progress from being made — family planning education.

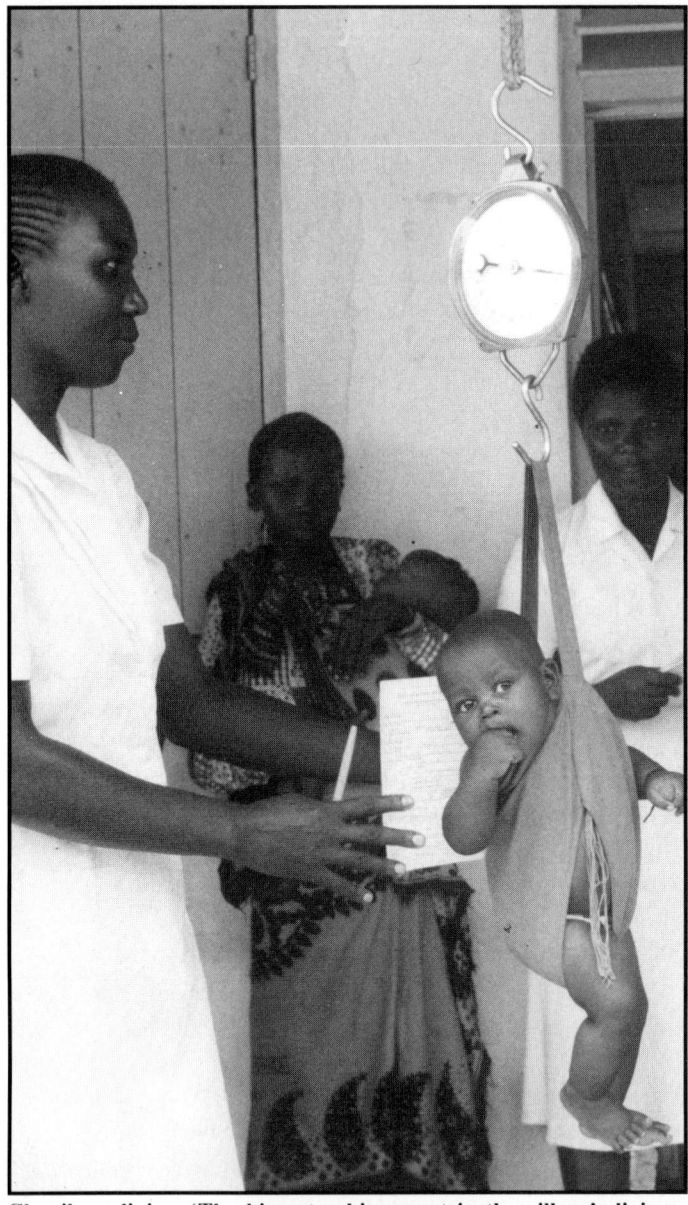

Chanika clinic: 'The biggest achievement in the village's living memory.'

TANZANIA: A life-saving clinic in remote Chanika

Workers at the clinic admit that they have not succeeded in persuading men and women to discuss their family planning problems. "They feel ashamed and totally reserved," says Stella Makwabe, the clinic staff nurse. "Although we have done all we can, they won't budge."

A random survey has shown that most families in the village have between 5 and 10 children. And the mothers do not seem worried although they are the most affected. "I have no limit, I would have 10 children and more," says Amina Salum, who is already a mother of eight.

The lack of a comprehensive family planning programme for Tanzania's villages is putting a strain on the overburdened national economy. The central committee of the ruling party, Chama Cha Mapinduzi (the Revolutionary Party of Tanzania), has directed the government to initiate a programme to check the growing population. Finance Minister, Cleopa Msuya, has pointed out that the population passed the 23 million mark in 1981, rising from the 12 million of 1967. "This is a very dangerous signpost," he has warned.

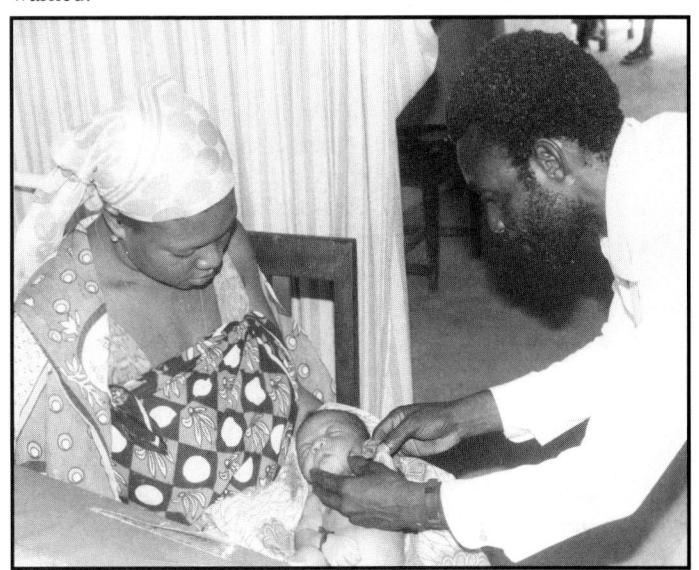

The clinic has saved the lives of many children.

Dumping ground

By the time the clinic was completed in 1976 Chanika had attracted more than 4,000 residents and the number kept increasing. By 1982, the village had 6,000 people.

In 1985, when John Mhaville was appointed as the new Regional Commissioner for Dar es Salaam, the "back-to-the-land" campaign had lost its impetus; in the capital, the population had risen to 1.8 million compared with an estimated 1.2 million in 1980.

So Mhaville launched his own campaign, popularly known as "Operation Vijiji" (Operation Villagisation), directed at the unemployed who were then estimated by the Home Affairs Ministry to be around 20%.

Chanika once again became a dumping ground for the city's "undesirables", and as the population grew to 10,000 the existing facilities were no longer able to cope.

Dr Mmboma says the clinic was intended to cater for a total of 4,000 people. The population increase has put immense pressure on his staff of two auxiliaries, two nurses and a ward attendant. "This is too much for us," he complains, adding that the Health Ministry had no contingency plans to deal with the situation because the country was short of medical personnel in all departments.

The Ministry's Director of Manpower Development, Dr Kitindi Kumpuni, says the shortage of personnel should ease over the next five years. "There has not been any proper assessment of manpower needs," he admits, but insists that the ministry will train enough people to meet the needs of the hospitals and health centres.

He blames the shortage on the "unplanned" and unexpected increase in the number of hospitals and health centres. "We probably would do better to co-ordinate people's efforts with those of the central government," he says, suggesting that Chanika-type self-help schemes, although laudable, could be catastrophic without co-ordinated planning.

The government is now planning to train two people in primary health care from every village across the country in order to achieve its target of "health for all" by the year 2000.

TANZANIA: A life-saving clinic in remote Chanika

Expedit Ibibya, the rural medical aide, goes around the village once every month to attend to the sick who are unable to visit the clinic.

But so far the government's role in Chanika has been insignificant — at least in the opinion of the villagers who cannot remember help ever being given in times of need.

Government assistance has been limited to the fight against malaria, which the villagers agree had threatened to become permanent. Medicine for this has been supplied from central stores and a small dispensary has been set up near the clinic.

To ease overcrowding at the clinic, Chanika officials have decided to decentralise the village health services. The village covers 25 square kilometres (15.5 square miles) and three makeshift centres have been established within this area.

Again this was done by the villagers themselves who used trees and grass as building materials. "We hope to transform these into primary health posts," says Dr Mmboma. "We are now giving vaccinations against cholera and hope the programme will be in full swing in the next six months."

Chanika's strength lies in the villagers' self-reliance. Village elder Said Geshi says the attitude of self-help is so deeply ingrained that "nobody here ever dreams of having a godfather".

"We did not look to a big brother when we drew up this self-help project," he explains. And this is true. Even the CDTF only became involved to support efforts already being made by the people of Chanika.

Projecting to 1990

Lucius Ikanda, the CDTF officer attached to the project, estimates that by 1990 the village will have 15,000 people, and possibly more if the present rate of settlement continues. "I predict disaster," he says. "Someone must stand up and call a halt to further developments that seem to be leading towards catastrophe." Village elder Lawrence Ifunga says the clinic has been "a saviour". But he wonders why no efforts are being made to expand it to prevent overcrowding as the population grows.

Apart from the clinic and dispensary, a primary school has been opened and officials say construction of a police station is imminent. "This time we must be ready for the population increase," says Emmanuel Chunda, the village secretary. "We must stop living like sardines."

Social workers and planners have not come up with any formula for tackling the problem. At first, resettlement of unemployed town dwellers was seen as a "necessary evil" to stem the urban population explosion. But although the resettlement campaigns have stopped, Chanika's population is still rising.

At the present rate of increase, the village will need twice its present health facilities by 1990, according to expert estimates.

Health Minister Dr Aaron Chiduo believes Chanika should close its doors to any new settlers. But this is a difficult decision to implement because under Tanzanian law the land belongs to everyone and remains under state control.

One option is for the village to apply to the Lands Ministry to extend its borders. But officials say this would commit the government to providing the necessary infrastructure within the new boundaries — the price of which would be high.

TANZANIA: A life-saving clinic in remote Chanika

The dispensary building: Shortage of medical personnel is a serious problem.

So villagers are now hoping to alleviate the problem by invoking by-laws as a deterrent to further population influx — village governments can pass laws and execute them provided they are endorsed by the Ministry for Regional Administration.

The population explosion has already affected the soil, which has been greatly over-used. The villagers do not understand the importance of rotational cultivation and the soil has become degraded. That has been made worse by indiscriminate felling of trees for firewood. Some trees had to be cleared to make room for the clinic but the crux of the problem is the lack of alternative energy sources for cooking and heating.

The village has no electricity and constant kerosene shortages force the people to burn firewood. "Our refrigerator will not work because we have no kerosene to fan it," complains a clinic attendant. The kerosene shortages frequently make it impossible for the clinic staff to carry out their vaccination programmes.

Lack of firewood near the village now makes it necessary for the women to walk long distances to find enough for cooking. And the same women also have to fetch water from distant parts of the village for washing and cooking.

Chanika has considered reapplying to CDTF for further support but the fund only has limited resources and all requests must go through the government. The villagers feel the procedure for securing a loan would take too long.

"We need time," says Frederick Ally, Planning Manager for CDTF projects in Tanzania. "We need time to scrutinise this and that and to conduct our own studies on project proposals. We can't help anyone who is in a hurry."

How does CDTF assess Chanika's past efforts? Executive Director Mathias Chonya describes Chanika as a "living testimony". He says: "It's one of the few villages that have taken the initiative to stand on its own feet".

Chonya believes that the government and all the development agencies should "show the way" to villagers in rural areas so that they themselves can direct development. "After all it's the wearer who knows where the shoe pinches," he says.

Development dangers

Chonya warns against "charity development" and "development by appeasement" which he says is ruinous and detrimental to the recipients.

"CDTF has done away with this kind of development aid. Our emphasis has shifted to participatory development where we require the beneficiaries of CDTF funds to show the initiative and identify the areas where they need help."

> *'Without this thing most of us would be gone.'*

Is the Chanika project sustainable? The villagers think so. "When the project was being conceived and when we were knocking on people's doors to mobilise their support, nobody realised the clinic would become such a symbol," says village chairman Makwaia Felix.

The project is sustainable because the villagers see it as their "salvation" and maintain it as their property. "Without this thing most of us would be gone," says one old woman in her seventies.

There is little doubt that the villagers are grateful to CDTF for encouraging their self-reliance, which has now become a firmly rooted tradition. The fund deserves credit for its long-term vision at a time when some governments and donor agencies are focusing on less sustainable projects like huge airports and highways that lead nowhere.

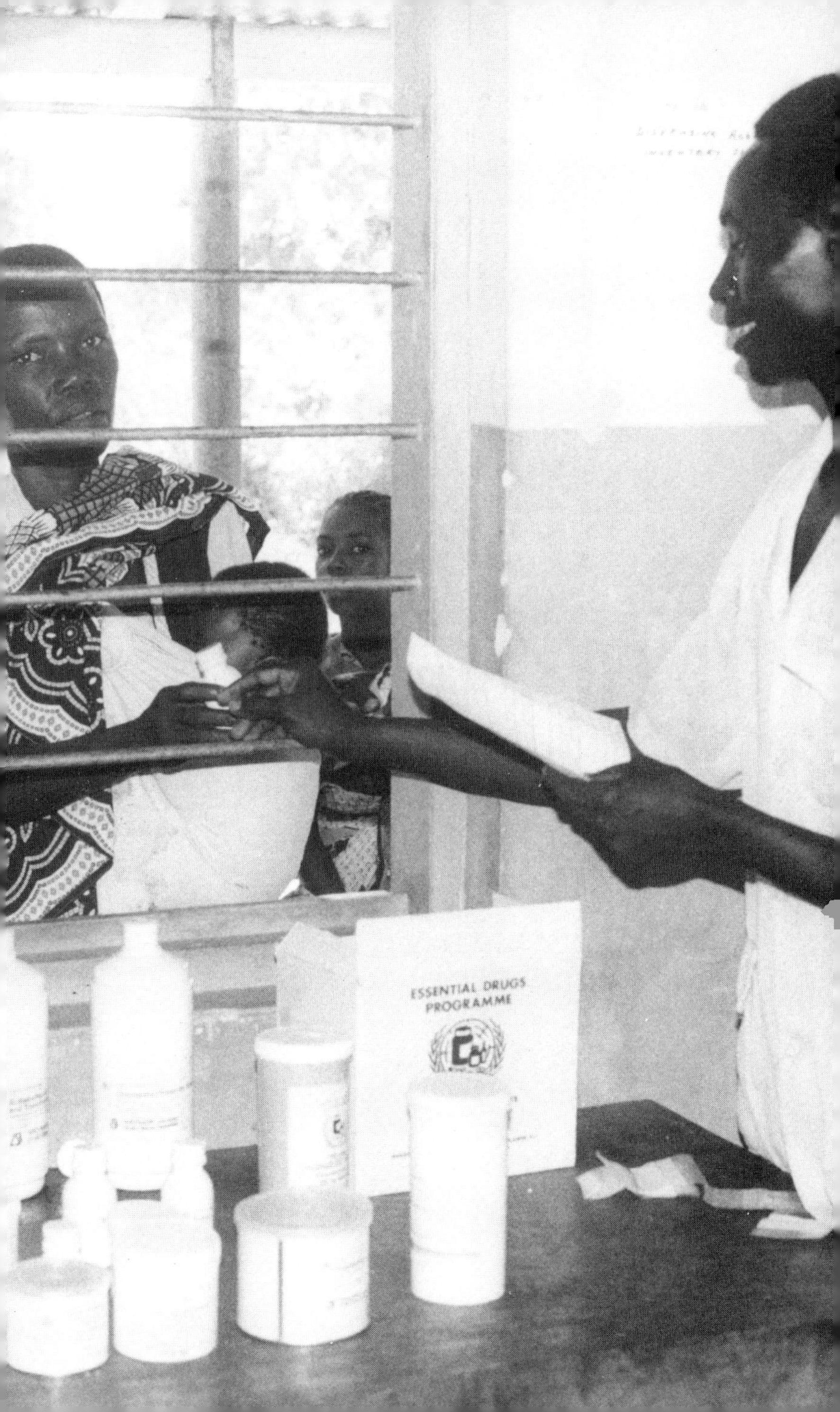
ESSENTIAL DRUGS
PROGRAMME

Perhaps the most vital lesson that governments and donors can learn from CDTF is that there are long-term benefits in building the confidence of communities so that they can do things for themselves.

It is this approach which has made the people of Chanika realise that they hold the key to their own future. As Makwaia Felix keeps telling his people: "It's small but it's home."

BANGLADESH

BREAKING THE
GRIP OF GREEDY
LANDOWNERS

NURUL HUDA

BANGLADESH: Breaking the grip of greedy landowners

NURUL HUDA

Development experts have been known to describe Bangladesh as a typical "international basket-case". In material terms, Bangladesh is indeed one of the world's poorest countries. It combines extreme poverty with the highest population density in the world: 103 million people occupy an area of about 143,000 square kilometres (55,000 square miles).

With a growth rate of 2.4% per year the population is likely to double within 30 years. The country has to wrestle with a grain deficit of up to 2 million tonnes annually; in 1987, another million was added to this figure when floods ruined the crops — and the deficit was higher in 1988, with even more devastating floods.

Yet amidst the gloom and despair, there are islands of hope which have been created by the work of non-governmental organisations. Small projects dotted throughout the country — large-scale ones too — tenaciously initiated by people, have risen against all odds.

Proshika, the Centre for Human Development, is one such organisation. Working quietly and patiently, away from the glare of the media, it has been mobilising landless farmers and helping them to improve their quality of life.

Fragile foundations

Proshika works mainly with subsistence farmers. In doing so, it has to reckon with Bangladesh's fragile agricultural foundations.

BANGLADESH: Breaking the grip of greedy landowners

Years of deforestation in the Himalayas have led to increased soil erosion, which in turn leads to the accumulation of silt along the beds of rivers entering Bangladesh. The major rivers within Bangladesh carry about 2.4 billion tonnes of sediment annually. Such incessant siltation without proper dredging of the waterways leads to widespread and frequent flooding, and large death tolls.

Even the dry months from November to March bring little respite. Then floods can be followed by devastating drought. Too much land is at the mercy of unreliable rainfall. Of the 13.2 million hectares (33 million acres) under crops in 1985-86, only 2.8 million hectares were watered by irrigation; the remainder depend entirely on rainfall.

Social and economic problems add to the difficulties. Agriculture is the mainstay of the economy: landlessness is one of the major causes of poverty. In the rural areas, where most of the population live, 10% of the families control 56% of the arable land. Conservative estimates suggest that no less than 51% of rural families are landless.

According to one survey, about half the people who are landless today lost their land over the last two decades. During droughts and famines, wealthy landowners stand outside the land registry offices

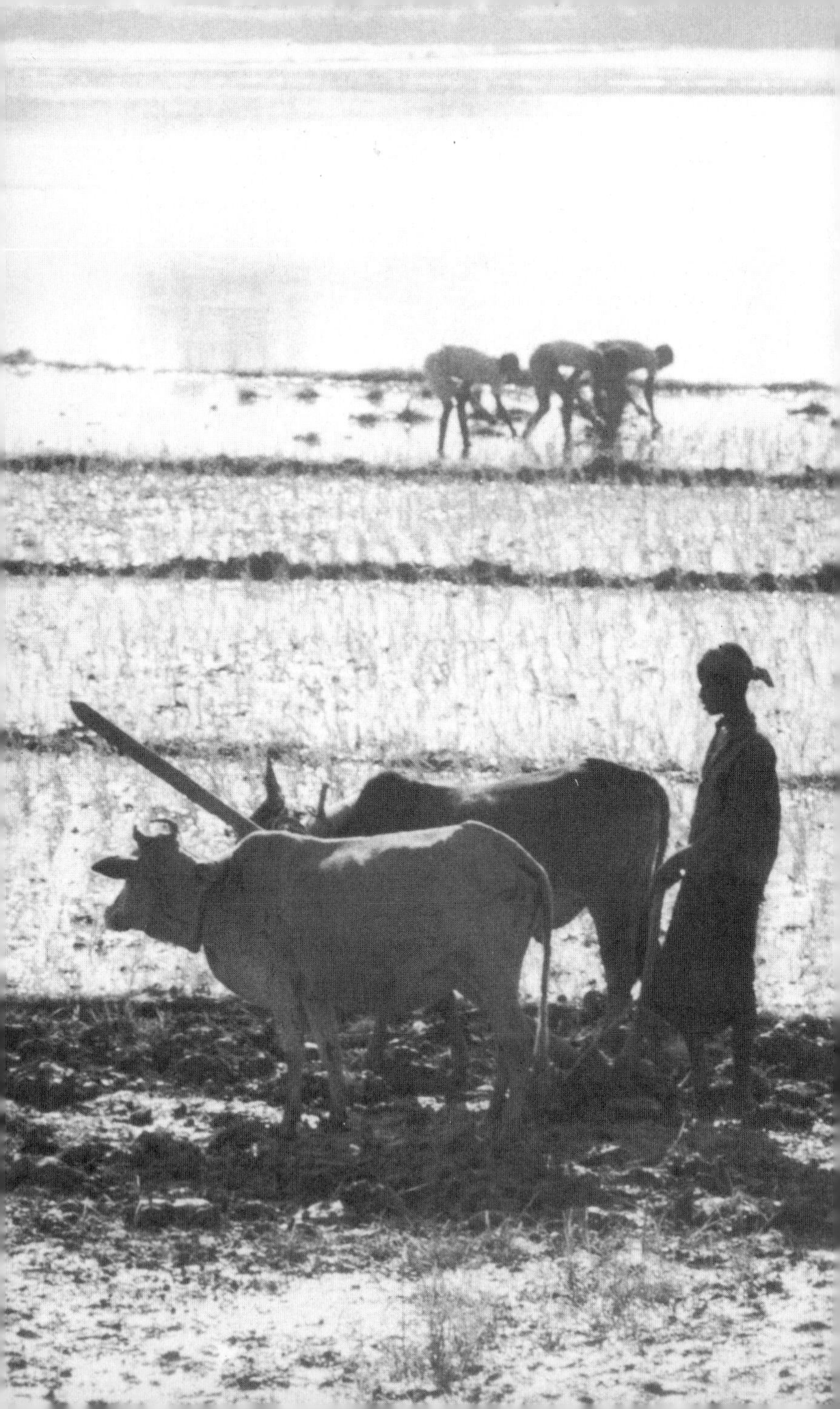

all day and night to snap up land sold for a pittance by desperate small farmers.

More than 80% of farms are less than two acres in size, most of them subsistence smallholdings. Of the total area under cultivation, 54% produces only one harvest a year, 38% two harvests, and only 8% is triple-cropped.

The government's approach

Expanding irrigation schemes to bring water to more areas is one of the government's top priorities. The policy includes developing appropriate water conservation and management programmes, improving the cropping pattern and intensity, excavating canals and dredging river beds.

The government is also determined to get more and more farmers to understand and apply modern methods. It is trying to achieve this by supplying materials such as fertiliser, improved seeds and irrigation equipment, and making credit more readily available.

The current five-year plan, for 1986-90, emphasises the rapid expansion of water facilities during the dry season in order to increase the output of crops such as paddy, wheat, pulses, oil seeds and vegetables.

The government's stated target is to increase grain production to 20.7 million tonnes by 1990, as compared to 16 million tonnes in 1986. It intends doing this by expanding the irrigation facilities. The aim by then is to irrigate 3.7 million hectares (9.2 million acres).

But government plans have run into a host of problems. At least half of the rural households are unable to make use of government assistance. They do not qualify for institutional credit at reasonable interest rates because they do not own the land needed as collateral to secure a loan.

Distribution of high-yielding seed varieties has been slow, and progress in expanding the area under irrigation has often been disrupted by farmers' lack of resources, and by conflicts with the big landowners who feel threatened by the possibility of the rural poor having control over irrigation schemes.

Agriculture is the mainstay of the Bangladeshi economy; landlessness is one of the major causes of poverty.

It is for such reasons that the amount of land under irrigation h~s increased at a snail's pace: from 9.1% in 1970-71 to 10.5% in 1979-80, according to official estimates. Unofficial estimates question even these figures.

A different way

This pathetic rate of progress convinced the government that an alternative approach had to be taken.

Starting in 1980, government authorities turned to the non-governmental organisations, like Proshika, to break through the impasse and set up imaginative and meaningful programmes to assist and include the rural poor.

Established in 1976, Proshika now operates in 22 of the country's 64 districts. Activities fall into four main categories: organising the rural poor; development education; creating employment and income- generating projects; and emergency relief and rehabilitation.

According to Kazi Farouque Ahmed, the Executive Director,

Proshika seeks "to help the rural groups to articulate their problems, as well as formulate programmes and action".

He goes on: "We believe that development is neither a dole nor the elusive growth and productivity measured in terms of input and output alone. Development is very much the people's business. Outside intervention and assistance are welcome as long as they help to break the dependency relations.

"People must be given the opportunity to think for themselves, speak for themselves, work for themselves, and even make mistakes by themselves."

'People must be given the opportunity to think for themselves, speak for themselves, work for themselves, and even make mistakes by themselves.'

Proshika's annual budget runs to more than Taka 30 million (US$1 million). Between 75% to 80% of the budget comes from the Swedish International Development Authority (SIDA), Novib of the Netherlands, and the Ford Foundation. The rest comes from its own income-generating activities. One major source of income is from its fleet of 12 passenger buses.

As it works closely with the rural poor, the administrative structure of Proshika is heavily decentralised. To maintain close links with rural life, it has set up development centres in 36 areas throughout Bangladesh. The Area Development Centres (ADCs), as they are called, serve mainly as bases from which field workers organise the groups they are trying to help. The centres also conduct training programmes.

Proshika's crucial part

Proshika's projects span a broad spectrum: irrigation, agriculture, reclamation of mortgaged land, cattle raising, poultry raising, rice milling, bee-keeping, rural industry and handicrafts, fish farming, silkworm breeding, plant nurseries, a rickshaw project and social forestry.

The projects are implemented by groups. Each group comprises between 15 and 20 people, who all come from similar social and economic backgrounds. Project personnel have found that similarity of occupation and social status are vital factors in the smooth running of the group and in its cohesion when under pressure.

Proshika has grown rapidly. By 1985, there were 664 employment and income-generating schemes.

Irrigation — the artificial application of water to land, especially for agriculture — accounts for 37% of Proshika's activities.

Large-scale irrigation projects have improved the ability to increase agricultural production in Bangladesh. They have also contributed towards increasing the income of some people.

But as in many other parts of the world, there are social, political and environmental problems: deterioration of soil through salinisation and waterlogging; depletion of groundwater resources; the spread of water-borne diseases; the increased use of pesticides; the deterioration of fisheries; the forced displacement of communities; and excessive costs in relation to economic returns.

Above all, irrigation projects have mainly benefited the rich landowners who control the water pumps and have the resources to buy fertilisers and pesticides, and the ability to make use of government subsidies.

Proshika's irrigation efforts are more modest. The organisation believes that efficient and sustainable irrigation depends on a combination of four basic factors: availability of capital; a reliable and equitable supply of water; adequate incentive for farmers; and an adequate flow of technical information.

Kazi Farouque Ahmed, Executive Director, Proshika.

In 1980, the organisation launched its first irrigation projects. The results were positive. With the government's financial support, they now operate 241 irrigation projects with the help of landless farmers.

"The whole point of these irrigation schemes is that they should serve as the means whereby irrigation technology gets into the hands and falls under the control of the landless and landpoor in Bangladesh," says Mahbubul Karim, a Proshika senior official.

He explains that the schemes were an attempt to help the landless agricultural labourers and marginal farmers to acquire and run mechanised irrigation equipment themselves. The equipment includes: low lift pumps to use water from ponds or rivers; shallow tubewells to draw water from the first underground water sources; deep tubewells that go down between 30 to 70 metres to exploit lower water levels. The poor would then be in a position to sell water to large landowners and cultivators.

"It is in fact a move to prevent the rich landowners from also

Proshika's projects help poor farmers to acquire and run mechanised irrigation equipment themselves.

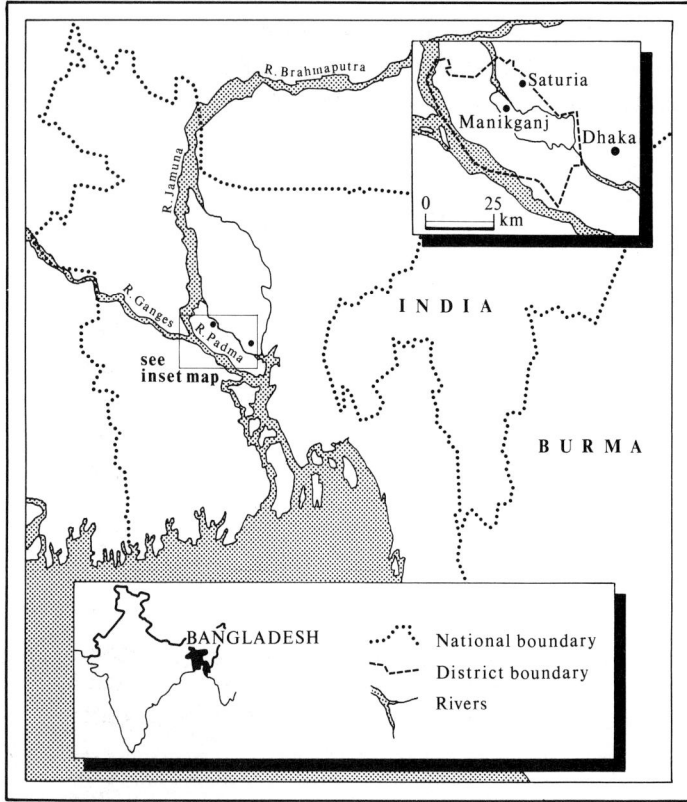

Manikganj district

becoming water-lords, who would monopolise this crucial means of production," he says.

According to Kazi Khaze Alam, Proshika's programme co-ordinator, Bangladesh still has rural property rights, other than land rights, from which landless people can derive rent and a consequent improvement in their social status.

"These irrigation schemes are also proving that loans can quite safely be extended to the poor without having to demand land from them as collateral," he says.

In the formative stages of the irrigation projects, Proshika arranges bank loans by guaranteeing 50% of the credit, and helps with the purchase of irrigation equipment.

About 2,400 hectares (6,000 acres) have been brought under irrigation as a result of the projects. The families of about 3,600 group members have benefited directly or indirectly.

The projects have created employment for about 400 group members, giving them work as engine drivers for about six months of the year. Furthermore, over two dozen mechanics have been trained and now sell their maintenance skills to owners and users of irrigation equipment.

What is particularly noteworthy is that the repayment/recovery rate of all types of loans to people who previously had no savings at all is estimated by Proshika to be nearly 80%.

From the general to the particular: the details of the Proshika project at Atigram provide an illuminating case study ...

ATIGRAM: an irrigation case study

Name of project: *Atigram Garib Unnyan Sanchayee Samity (Atigram Development Savings Society for the Poor)*
Tier of local government: *Village and Union Parishad (lowest tier) Atigram*
Upazila — Basic unit of administration: *Saturia*
District of Bangladesh: *Manikganj*
Date when samity formed: *10 September 1979*
Number of members: *20 (began with 18)*
When irrigation project launched: *1980-81*
Project area: *Over 15 acres (6 hectares) in 1986-87*
Initial project area: *10 acres (4 hectares)*
Number and type of engine: *One shallow tubewell*
Wages during harvesting season: *Tk 30-35 (US$1) per day*
Number of farmers: *16*
Farmers cultivating own land: *8 who own 10 acres in the project area*
Number of share-croppers (tenants): *4, cultivating 2 acres of others' land in the command area*
Other farmers: *4 who own 3 acres.*

Villagers in Atigram discuss problems of common concern.

How it began

Mohidur Rahman, a Proshika field worker, visited the village and met with 18 young men. He assured them that Proshika would co-operate with them in their efforts to improve the quality of their lives.

A few months after the "samity" (a society) was formed, the members discussed with Rahman the possibility of getting an irrigation project going in the village. He told them that, if they were determined and didn't give up halfway through, there was no reason why they could not get a useful scheme underway. He helped them to prepare the outlines of the project.

When they felt sufficiently confident that the scheme they had in mind was viable, some members of the samity approached the farmers of the village and discussed the project with them. Rahman was asked to be present at that meeting.

The landless labourers debated the pros and cons of the proposed project with the farmers, who had good reason to pay attention. They had long been at the mercy of nature's storms and droughts and had frequently lost crops to floods. They therefore responded favourably. The only reservation the farmers had was born of traditional attitudes to landless people. The landless had been regarded as people without roots, and therefore without a stake in property or a long-term commitment to improving the countryside. The farmers had grave doubts about the ability of the landless to implement and run an expensive irrigation project. But the farmers had no alternative. Either they threw in their lot with the peasants, or they would remain vulnerable to drought.

After much discussion and thought, the landless villagers and the farmers signed a five-year agreement fixing the price which the farmers would pay for water supplied by the irrigation project.

> *'Our earnings from this project have released us from our misery. We are now eating much better — two meals a day.'*

The farmers agreed to pay one-third of the crops as water charges. They also undertook to improve productivity and increase the yield. Should the plot of land concerned be handed over to share-croppers for cultivation, the farmers were obliged to ensure that the terms of the agreement were still complied with.

For its part, the samity committed itself to ensuring the supply of water during the relevant seasons, for which it was given the right to dig drains as and where necessary. The samity also agreed that in the event of trouble with the diesel engine or breakdown of the pump, it would undertake repairs immediately.

Project approval

Such agreements are a prerequisite of project approval by Proshika. The project proposal has to carry a copy of the agreement, a sketch map of the plots involved in the project, as well as the names and signatures of the farmers concerned.

Having been given the go-ahead by Proshika, the proposal had to be approved by the local government irrigation committee. This was necessary to secure a bank loan to purchase a pump for the Atigram samity. The samity also signed another agreement with Proshika, undertaking to repay the loan within the stipulated time.

After the paperwork was sorted out, work on the project began.

The Atigram project has facilitated a much more efficient use of water by distributing it more fairly to both small farmers and the landless.

Samity members worked with Proshika staff to install the shallow tubewell. Although the villagers had never come across such equipment before, the scheme has brought about a much more efficient use of water by distributing it more fairly and systematically to both small farmers and share croppers.

After some months, the samity decided to reduce the water

BANGLADESH: Breaking the grip of greedy landowners

Access to a continuous water supply has enabled small farmers to grow two crops a year.

charges to counteract competition from the installation of irrigation equipment by big landowners in the area. It slashed the water charges from one-third of the crops to one-quarter, which pleased the small farmers.

Three years after the project was launched, the samity paid back the loans. During the 1986-87 season, each member of the society earned a profit of Tk1,500 (US$50) — equivalent to 360 kilogrammes of paddy. The members are now the sole owners of the irrigation equipment.

For Salam, the engine driver, the project has guaranteed him a job for six months of the year. Previously, he had no regular source of income. In the 1986-87 season, he earned Tk3,000 (US$95) in wages, in addition to the paddy he received as a member of the society, which enabled him to feed his family for four months.

The project has changed the attitudes of small farmers and share croppers. It has improved the quality of their lives and made them realise that they can change difficult situations through their own efforts.

Access to a continuous water supply has enabled small farmers to grow two crops during the year. Many farmers now grow high-yielding rice varieties in one crop and traditional varieties like "aus" and "aman" in the next.

Says Rabindranath, a small farmer: "The project has freed me from the chains of the money-lenders by enabling me to earn more. I used to borrow money by mortgaging family brassware items at very high rates of interest — simply to meet the costs of basic necessities. There used to be no escape from the money-lenders after my family had spent days with no food at all to eat."

He adds: "Our earnings from this project have released us from our misery. We are now eating much better — two meals a day. We've bought three calves from the money we managed to save and we make a monthly contribution of Tk5 to the samity fund."

Proof of sustainability

Despite the difficulties encountered and the lack of experience of the samity members when they started, the project has been running for seven years — proof of its sustainability. And this sustainability is based precisely on the members' belief that they have managed to improve their lives by pooling their efforts.

Their plans to buy more engines, their moves to counter the

tactics of the big landowners, and the willingness with which they do voluntary labouring work, are all signs that the members have no intention of abandoning this project which promises to improve their conditions even more in the future.

Indeed it has become clear that the Atigram irrigation project can survive even if Proshika does not continue to lend it the funds to meet the operating costs. Such a contingency would, however, entail economic hardship for the members. Nevertheless, they have established goodwill in the community and proved their loan-worthiness. If necessary, they could, they say, meet the operational costs partly by borrowing and partly by using the proceeds from the sale of their cattle.

The whole purpose of the project has been environmental in the sense that it involves reducing people's vulnerability to the vagaries of nature. By digging drains and clearing canals and pumping water where required, the members of the project have to some extent made the land more hospitable and productive. The project has brought about a better and more equitable use of water resources in the area.

It is evident that the rate of economic return varies from plot to plot and from one year to the next, depending on the yield that is coaxed from the land. While not sensationally attractive, the project's rate of return has been good enough to encourage the members to further efforts.

Possible improvements

The most obvious way in which the project could be improved is by expanding the irrigated area. For this, a more powerful engine must be installed. This is now very much in the minds of the members.

Extension of electricity to the project site would substantially reduce operating costs. So would operation of the engine, to some extent at least, on a voluntary basis. Availability of spare parts and fuel, in the locality, and greater technical support would further improve efficiency.

"More frequent meetings with farmers to advise them on the

AGAINST ALL ODDS

Rabindranath, a small farmer, with his new acquisition, bought from the money he had saved.

proper use of inputs would improve the project's rate of return," says Ashrafuddin Biswas, a Proshika worker. "They should also be helped to take appropriate measures, and at the right time, to minimise the damage to the crops caused by pests."

But not all Proshika irrigation projects have worked. Kazi Alam, the project co-ordinator, readily admits that about 11 have had problems.

Jealousy among samity members has been a major problem at times. There were also ugly confrontations with big farmers who installed irrigation equipment close to the water pumps run by the landless in the project areas.

Excessive seepage of water due to sandy soil and floods damaged several projects. Violation of the terms of the loan agreements led to the collapse of some schemes.

Babul Krishna, one of the co-ordinators in charge of the irrigation programme, lists other factors too: "Breakdown of the engines driving the pumps and damage caused by fire immediately after installation have demoralised some of the members sufficiently to make them give up in despair. Depletion of the sub-soil water table, irregularities in the way accounts are kept, and poor participation when voluntary labour is required, have also brought some schemes to grief. In one area an engine driver was killed, while in another project the engine itself was actually stolen."

Other detrimental factors

Mustafizur Rahman, a graduate in irrigation and water management, and now responsible for extending Proshika's irrigation programme, focuses on still other aspects.

"At the beginning, the selection of sites for some of the projects was wrong," he points out. "Approval was given to such projects without a proper feasibility study having been carried out beforehand. But we have learnt from these experiences and the projects launched more recently are doing better."

Projects in different parts of the country have suffered from a number of other factors: the scattered location of farm holdings; lack of adequate equipment; delays in implementation; starting projects in the wrong season; and the poor water-retaining capacity of the soil. Sometimes these factors have acted singly, sometimes in combination with one or two other negative contingencies.

Faulty construction of drains has also at times undermined the commitment of some members.

Several projects have had to cope with excessive seepage from drains; supply of much more water than required; non-availability of water when it is required; lack of proper engine maintenance; and failure of the engine to work according to its stated capacity.

However, Proshika's overall experience, particularly in Atigram, shows that even the poorest and most neglected sections of society are capable of contributing to important development programmes, given the necessary guidance, training and support. They are capable in due course of providing leadership themselves and of playing a major role in the nation's production system.

What should not be forgotten, however, is the crucial support of Proshika at every stage of the project's development. It is true to say that without the encouragement and advice of this NGO, the projects would not have got started in the first place.

KENYA

THE PARKING BOYS
OF NAIROBI

DOROTHY MUNYAKHO

KENYA: The parking boys of Nairobi

DOROTHY MUNYAKHO

A boy emerges from an alley adjacent to Tom Mboya Street in Nairobi, Kenya's capital. He is carrying a bundle of waste paper collected from dustbins and is hurrying to a middleman who will buy the paper and in turn sell it to a recycling plant.

The boy's name is Chesire Barasa Thomas. He looks no more than 13. He does not know his exact age. He dropped out of school when he was too young to remember such details because his father, a labourer on a coffee farm, couldn't afford the fees. He has been collecting waste paper because he needs the money to buy sugar and soap for his mother, younger brother and sister.

Chesire is just one of thousands of children of school age who have been driven by poverty into the streets of Nairobi. They eke out a living doing anything that is likely to bring in a few shillings — rummaging through garbage for items that could conceivably be saleable and going to the wholesale market, the "marikiti", where they pick up the odd tomato or potato left behind in the course of transactions.

Some sing for a living on the pavements of the city, or resort to begging, imploring passers-by to spare them a coin.

Others, when all else has failed, embark on more daring ventures like shoplifting, or trying to pick the pockets of people who look well-off and incapable of catching them. Gradually, with each small success, they slide into a life of petty theft and casual crime.

KENYA: The parking boys of Nairobi

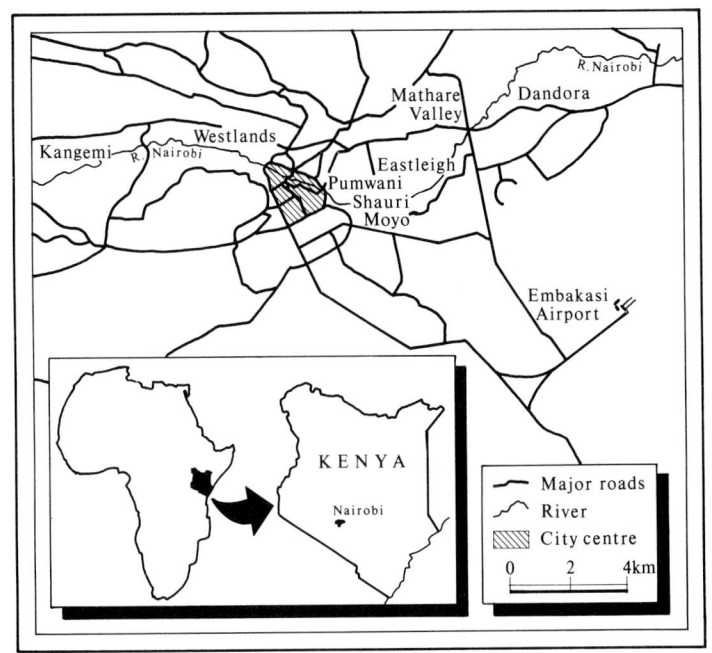

Nairobi

The term, "parking boys", is used for Nairobi's street children: it derives from one of their popular activities, which is directing motorists to available parking spaces along crowded kerbs during peak hours. The children guard the cars until the drivers return. Their tips depend on the generosity of the drivers.

The problem of neglected children, both boys and girls, is not restricted to Nairobi. There are large numbers of them in urban centres throughout Kenya, especially Mombasa, Kisumu and Nakuru.

A worldwide problem

In fact, the problem of street children is worldwide. There are an estimated 100 million, most of them in the South.

Asia and Latin America are believed to have the largest numbers. But Africa, whose population is currently growing more rapidly than any other region, could well have the greatest number of destitute children by the year 2000. Thus, the fact that Kenya has

Nairobi's "parking boys" rummaging through garbage in search of saleable items.

fewer children on the streets of its major towns at present than do Asian and Latin American cities, is no reason for complacency.

A non-governmental organisation, known as the Undugu Society of Kenya, has been concerned about the country's parking boys ever since it was formed in 1975 specifically to deal with that problem. Fabio Dallape, director of Undugu, fears that there is a real danger of the number of Nairobi street children increasing up to 20-fold by the turn of the century.

Dallape, a sociologist who has headed Undugu since 1977, argues that the problem of street children has deeper ramifications than simply the number of minors roaming around without adult supervision. He notes that the number of children actually visible in the main streets of Nairobi has decreased noticeably in recent times because they are facing competition in their struggle for survival from older youths and even adults.

"The children aren't fools," he says. "When they see there are no pickings left for them because of the pressure of people stronger than they are, they go and find hunting grounds elsewhere in the city. Officially, we are talking about 30,000 boys and girls who really ought to be in school. If at any particular time they aren't visible to the eye, it means they're doing their thing, working their schemes, in some out-of-the-way place."

National policy and street reality

Eliud Ngala Mwenda, chairman of the City Commission of Nairobi, stresses that the problem of street children is "serious" and "needs to be thought about carefully by all those individuals and organisations who feel its dimensions are getting out of control and that something has to be done about it".

The law in Kenya has long stated that it is illegal to mistreat dependent children. In terms of the Children and Young Persons Act it is an offence for parents "wilfully" to assault, ill- treat, neglect or abandon their children. Parents who neglect and abandon their children are liable to arrest without warrant.

What normally happens is that the police round up children who seem to be loitering and wandering about aimlessly and get the Children's Department to locate their parents. If and when the parents are found, they are required to sign a bond undertaking that for a specified period of time, their children will not be involved in the kinds of activities they were engaged in when the police brought them in.

The law applies to street children and to all under-age victims of neglect and abuse. But although a legal framework does exist to guard against situations which induce children to take to the streets, such children are just as ubiquitous and noticeable as the cars from which they try to make a living.

The underlying causes

The ineffectiveness of the law stems from its failure to recognise the stark poverty which drives parents, who might well love their children, to neglect, ignore and finally abandon them. "The commission's view is that tactics such as forcefully removing the kids from the streets are not solutions at all and have no hope of solving the problem in the long term," says Mwendwa.

Having left their villages with their families as a result of land degradation, many of the boys end up on the streets of Nairobi.

Every year about 3,000 children are left to fend for themselves when their mothers are arrested and sent to jail. By the time the mothers leave prison, many of their children will have got into the habit of scouring the streets in search of something to eat, companionship, and a place to sleep near their stamping ground when exhaustion overtakes them.

The fact that children drift onto the streets because of the lack of adult supervision, and not to enjoy themselves, highlights the superficiality of focusing on the symptoms of the problem. What this means is that simply rounding up the children by force time and time again is not really a way of dealing with the problem.

Mwendwa calls for "lasting solutions", which require a more fruitful line of action. He believes that finding places for the parking boys in schools, polytechnics and literacy centres would be far more effective and have more beneficial results.

But he is aware that some children on the loose will not respond appropriately. They will not meekly hand themselves over to people in authority, having developed a self-reliance in which trust in adults — grown-ups who have previously neglected, harmed, and abandoned them, and who keep rounding them up against their will — is a sign of foolishness.

Now it is the policy of the Nairobi City Commission to go to the roots of the problem — to look at the underlying causes which drive the children onto the streets. When these are understood, the chances of dealing with the problem are likely to be greater.

'Undugu' — brotherhood

"Undugu" is the Ki-Swahili word for "brotherhood" or "solidarity", and it has strong connotations with the Christian precept of charity, of being one's brother's keeper. Its philosophy is based on three principles: respect, work and service.

The society works with an annual budget of Kenya shillings 15 million (US$937,500). It has developed from being almost a one-man show into a well- recognised and independent national organisation.

The origins of Undugu go back to late in 1972 when Father Arnold Grol, a Dutch missionary, arrived in Nairobi. He noticed the large number of children roaming the streets and sitting on the pavements, unoccupied in any useful way.

"I started meeting the boys in Uhuru (freedom) Park, and giving them items of clothing donated by well-off people," Grol recalls. "But it soon

Father Arnold Grol, the founder and chairman of Undugu Society.

became clear that the boys wanted more than clothing. They said they wanted to learn things, like the kids who were lucky enough to be in school."

Grol approached another Hollander, Father Joseph Donders, who was then head of the Department of Philosophy and Religious Studies at the University of Nairobi. Donders agreed to let the boys be taught at the University Chapel.

> *'It soon became clear that the boys wanted more than clothing. They said they wanted to learn things, like the kids who were lucky enough to be in school.'*

This was how Undugu's programme of informal education and training got started in 1975. Today, the society runs four schools where the focus of attention is on self-development, rather than on "academic" subjects with which to attain a school certificate.

The curriculum at Undugu's Basic Education School in the Mathare Valley — designed in conjuction with the Kenya Institute of Education — is almost entirely practical. It is aimed at helping the children to become useful members of society by imparting technical skills which enable them to earn a living, and by influencing their attitudes.

Undugu's other three schools are in heavily-populated areas in Nairobi, and cater for some 450 pupils with a staff of 25 teachers.

Involving the community

Undugu's experience with slum children has brought Grol, who is chairman both of the society and of its board of trustees, to the conclusion that "you cannot educate children without involving their parents". Says programmes co-ordinator Ezra Mbogori: "Our target group has expanded to include slum dwellers as a whole".

The change of approach is a result of the bitter lessons learnt from the early days when Grol used to drive along the streets and load parking boys into his station wagon with the promise of food and shelter.

That way of proceeding had the effect of undermining the children's sense of doing things for themselves. It inculcated an attitude of dependency in street boys which served to discredit Undugu in the eyes of the community — and in the eyes of the parking boys themselves, who felt that the organisation had betrayed their expectations of it.

Take Abdi Ismail for instance. This parking boy absconded from Undugu because of what he calls "inhuman treatment" —"I didn't go to Undugu to dig but to be fed and to learn," he says.

The digging is an allusion to a piece of land Undugu bought in Katangi, 130 kilometres (80 miles) east of Nairobi with the aim of settling parking boys as farmers. The project failed because most parking boys are born in Nairobi and prefer to remain in the city. Migration from rural areas to towns is a major problem in Kenya; getting street boys to settle as farmers was out of the question.

It is not clear when Abdi quit Undugu. What matters is that Undugu has realised the futility of any approach which simply doles out charity. The society now accepts that the only method with any hope of success is one which cultivates in the children a sense of dignity and a pride in their ability to stand on their own feet.

Abdi ran away from Undugu's protection because he had thought that Undugu was a haven for destitutes where food and shelter came freely.

Eroding the combative spirit

"It appears that, whenever we take boys into an institution, even into a small home like we always will have, it takes away from them combativity for their own lives," director Dallape says. "In the streets, they have to fight for their survival. When they come to us, they stop fighting, and that is the danger."

Unlike children in normal families who are provided for by their parents and are expected in turn to study and to be obedient, children in institutional homes consider everything they receive as free. "The money you got is ours," is their attitude.

"We spoil them," Dallape says. "Yes, we get the money from donors, but instead of that money helping us to educate them, it becomes a weapon which they use to kill their own character."

Undugu projects are continually under trial. One course of action which the society tried for a while, as a way of not blunting the edge of children's need, was to stop feeding them in school. "We don't give food any more in our four Undugu schools, and the poor boys and girls are there from 9 am to 4 pm. Some cannot come anymore because they are hungry," says Grol.

Further experience, and changed conditions, persuaded Undugu to go back to giving some food to the children at its schools.

In the newest school, run by older slum boys who have had more learning, the boys collect items like scrap iron and waste paper in the morning; they sell these to buy food, and then attend school from 2 to 5 in the afternoon.

And whereas it used to be Undugu's practice to go out and pick up loitering children, more and more boys are now coming in on their own initiative after learning of the society's existence and how it might be able to change their lives.

Becoming part of the community

In 1987, in order to become an integral part of the community it seeks to serve, Undugu closed its reception centre in Westlands, a posh residential area of Nairobi with a high-class shopping complex.

"We closed the centre because it was odd, and completely out of place," Dallape says. "The children were surrounded by the rich and the only place they could get friendship and sympathy was at the market, in the streets or at Kanemi (the nearest slum estate)."

The centre was moved to the impoverished Dandora estate on the northeast side of the city: "We think the Dandora environment is much better than Westlands. We want our social workers and those in charge of the parking boys programme to meet the children where they are and do something for them where they live."

Underlining the importance of community involvement in the programme, Rich Maina, 33, the parking boys co-ordinator, reinforces Dallape's reasons for closing down the Westlands centre. It was ideal as a catchment area, he notes, as it was barely

KENYA: The parking boys of Nairobi

Undugu's offices, deliberately located in the slum areas, making them part of the people whom they serve.

three kilometres (1.8 miles) from the city centre haunts of the boys.

"But the children had no interaction with the community. Westlands people wanted to be on their own, and we thought the boys would be better off in Dandora, where they would interact with other boys in the community," Maina says.

Undugu's new commitment to the community it is serving is evident from the location of its various projects. The head office is in Shauri Moyo, probably Nairobi's oldest low-income estate and overlooking dilapidated railway quarters. The shelter-upgrading project has an office in Kitui Village, overlooking Shauri Moyo from the banks of the badly polluted Nairobi River. The site of the shelter-upgrading is at Pumwani, another down-market area, between Eastleigh and Shauri Moyo. The Eastleigh community home for boys lies across the road from the Mathare Valley, which is Nairobi's worst slum area, and there are two other homes in Dandora.

The advantage of housing parking boys within their kind of environment is that it allows for participation by the wider

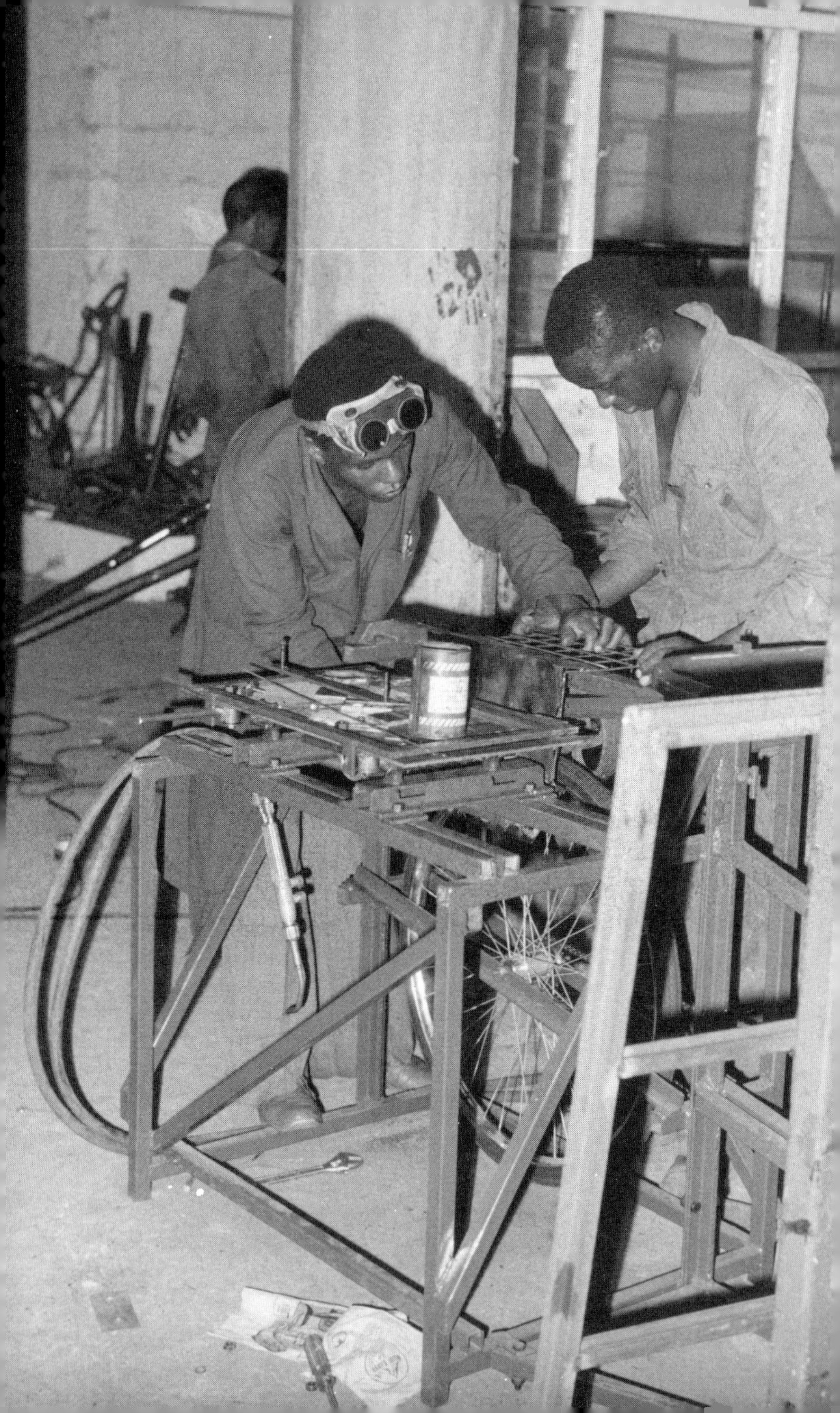

community as there are no barriers of social class to create unwanted tensions.

Nine-member committee

The parking boys programme has a nine-member committee which assists in investigating cases. The committee includes members of small Christian communities and, often, relatives of the boys already in the programme.

The boys include:
- Ernest Maina, aged 16, whose parents originally came from Murang'a, a rural area, where they could no longer support themselves on their small agricultural plot. Undugu pays Ernest's fees and gives him food and clothing.
- Joseph Kodoi, the latest arrival, ran away from home because his stepmother was ill-treating him; his father, a watchman, did nothing to stop her. Undugu has made arrangements for him to go to school.
- Vincent Adrian's father, is a German seaman who is known only as Martin. Vincent's mother has no land, and the boy came under the care of Undugu in 1982. The International Red Cross is helping to locate the father. Meanwhile, Vincent is studying for his Primary Education Certificate and says that, when he grows up, he wants to be a doctor.

Encouraging independence

In treating its parking boys programme as a process whereby the children are weaned from reliance on others and encouraged to become independent. Undugu gives them a weekly allowance: the children are left to manage the money for themselves, thus having to plan the food they will buy for the next seven days.

Once the boys are 17 or 18 years old, they are encouraged to live on their own. Undugu rents out a small room which two or three of them may share, and they receive an allowance for six months, by which time they are supposed to be self-supporting.

"That way, you have enabled them to face the realities of the harsh environment they are in," co-ordinator Mbogori says.

Nevertheless, the boys' spirit of independence does not usually carry them beyond the desire to become employed. Undugu would prefer more of the boys to become self-employed and truly self-sufficient, but most of them don't. The programme managers are aware that the majority of the boys they train aspire to academic certificates which will then, they hope, open the door to paid employment in the modern sector of the economy.

"Once they get their certificates, they would rather chase up jobs than set up a business in their own right," according to Mbogori. "Of every 15 boys trained by Undugu, 10 will go and look for jobs and only two will try to work for themselves."

The reason for this is that the trainees tend to be afraid to venture out on their own and to take their own risks. They prefer the security which they believe comes with a salary paid by someone else.

Pushed off the land

Most of Nairobi's slum dwellers, just like those in other developing countries, have migrated from rural areas where, like parents of many parking boys, they could no longer support themselves as a result of loss of their land, because of the arid conditions, or because the plots had become too small and unproductive to support all the members of their families.

Kenya's traditional land tenure system has never allowed women to inherit the land, although they are the country's main farmers. It is mainly for this reason that the women leave the rural areas when their fields can no longer feed them, and that something like 75% of the heads of households in the urban slums are women.

This means not only that more and more children in the rural areas are condemned to permanent landlessness, but also that most of the children roaming the urban streets will grow up to be unproductive unless some action is taken to improve the situation in the rural areas.

Only a relatively small number of people arriving in the city are simply attracted by the bright lights. What they have in common with all the other arrivals is their lack of skills and lack of work experience in the modern economy. If the landless are fortunate enough to find any paying job, they usually end up as casual labourers and the women, in particular, as servants.

At Undugu's Pumwani site, the society has launched a housing project to help the poor and to have an impact on the living conditions of children. James Kwangi, its co-ordinator, argues that if living standards in the slums are upgraded, the chances of children drifting into the streets will be lessened.

The project fits neatly into Kenya's housing policy. The country's current population is about 22 million and is growing at the very high rate of about 4% a year. To cope with the growth, along with overcrowding which already exists, and to replace the dwellings which cannot be improved, the government would have to build 87,000 units a year in urban areas, starting from 1985 and going through to the turn of the century.

At a cost of about Ksh60,000 (US$3,750) a house, this would require a budget in the region of Ksh80 billion (US$5 billion). But the slum dwellers cannot even afford to build houses that cost Ksh10,000 (US$625) each, according to Undugu's Ezra Mbogori. Hence Undugu's intervention in housing in 1983 when it provided the materials for people in Kitui village to build 250 basic dwellings, at a cost of about Ksh6,000 (US$375) each.

The residents cleared the land and prepared the sites and, under the guidance of a building supervisor, built their own single-room wattle-and-mud houses with corrugated iron roofs. A whole tract of land overlooking Shauri Moyo has been transformed by neat rows of houses of this kind. The residents also built a community hall and a nursery school. Soon after the houses had been put up, residents of neighbouring Kanuku asked for the same help, to replace their "igloos" — round hovels made of branches, plastic and cardboard. The residents of Kanuku lived in constant fear of their dwellings being razed by City Commission bulldozers in regular "cleaning-up" exercises.

The third Undugu housing project is at the adjacent village of Kinyago where the building of 318 houses, a nursery school and several shops, was completed in mid-1986. Undugu is now trying to persuade the city authorities to extend the sewerage system into the villages so that communal toilets can be built.

But there is a major stumbling block that has yet to be resolved: the provision of clean water. There is an underwater pipe through which the City Commission provides water to the community handpump. But the rate charged — 25 pennies (2 US cents) per 4-gallon jerrycan (about 18 litres) — is far too expensive for most people.

So the city supplies the water and charges it to the account of any local businessman who undertakes to pay the bills regularly. The catch is that the businessman then charges the locals double — 50 pennies per canful.

This situation forces most of the people in the area to draw their water from the heavily polluted Nairobi River. There are a number of concrete water containers on site to catch rainwater, but when it doesn't rain there is no alternative but to use the river water.

Attitude to donors

It is this range of experience that has enabled Undugu to say "no" to a donor organisation whose terms it considered to be incompatible with the realities in the slums of Nairobi. The organisation wanted its funds, raised from sponsoring families, to be used to improve the conditions of selected children. Undugu felt that such an individual focus would be "immoral" in a situation in which whole families were contributing help in a variety of ways.

After much discussion, the donor accepted Undugu's stand and only four out of the 240 sponsoring families withdrew from the programme ...

Undugu draws support from foreign donors. But it wants to reduce this dependence to an absolute minimum. This is considered desirable not only because it would give Undugu maximum control over its programmes, but would also enable it to finance innovative schemes, which may not attract donor support.

Two Undugu undertakings, the technical upgrading scheme and the retail crafts shop, are efforts in that direction. So is the depot from which quilts, baskets, and other homemade products are

KENYA: The parking boys of Nairobi

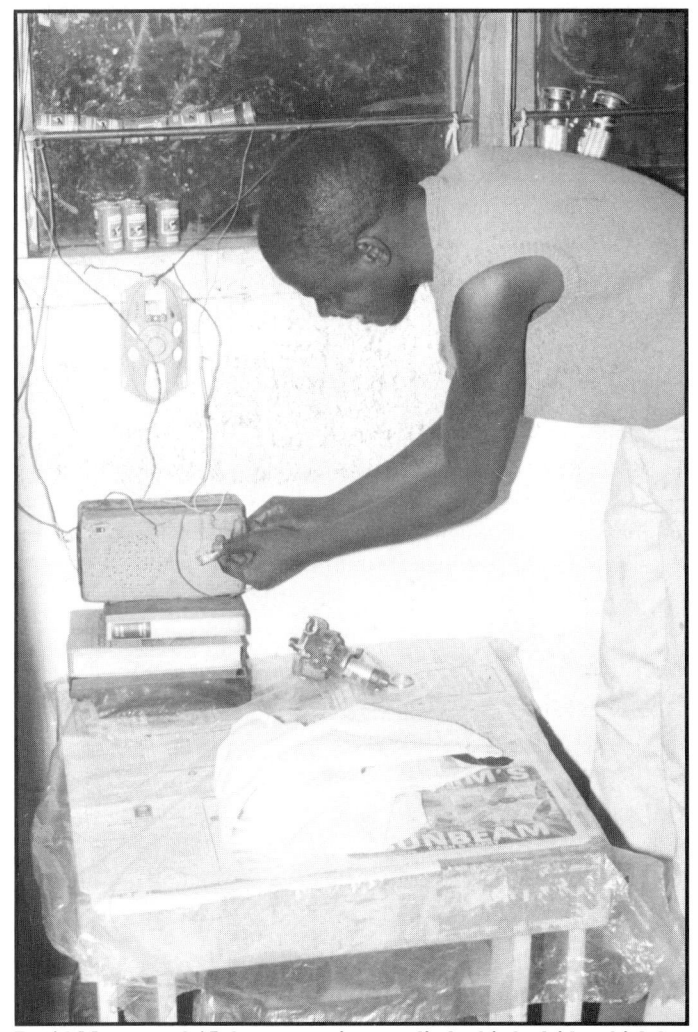

David Mutu, aged 15, has a transistor radio by his bedside which he has constructed himself.

exported to foreign markets. This unit was started in response to tourists' requests that goods be sent to addresses outside Kenya.

The Mathare Valley Women's Group, for example, produces patchwork quilts with original designs for which there is a big demand. The finished articles are sold through the Undugu shop in the premises of the old reception centre at Westlands. Curio shops in Nairobi also stock the women's products, as do retail outlets in some other countries in the South and in Europe, Canada and New Zealand.

"These are all income-generating activities whose profits are ploughed back into Undugu's operations," according to Mbogori.

Making a profit has never been an aim in itself, however. Profits simply provide Undugu with the means to do more.

Is Undugu successful?

The Undugu Society of Kenya has been grappling with a situation and with conditions that, over time, tend to undermine people's self-confidence and grind them down into resentment, apathy or crime. So the criteria by which its success is measured should be appropriate to the tough conditions, and should not simply reflect measures of success that are normally applied to development projects.

One measure of Undugu's success is the financial support it receives from the government. Also, the curriculum for its Basic Education School at Mathare Valley, designed with the help of the Kenya Institute of Education, has been formally recognised by the government.

The Kenya Government is also supporting Undugu by paying the salaries of slightly more than half of the teaching staff at the Basic Education School. The annual contribution towards the salaries comes to Ksh500,000 (US$31,250).

A valuable measure, too, is what former parking boys think of the programme ...

George Muhoro, aged 20, has been with Undugu since he was 13. He is now a carpenter's apprentice. He left school when his mother died and a brief stay with his grandmother convinced him that she was in no position to meet his needs. He then moved into the streets where he got caught up in the parking boys syndrome.

"I gathered scattered potatoes at the marikiti and sold them, I unscrewed the lamps on people's cars and sold them. I pounced on women at night and snatched their money and anything else they had," he says.

Almost inevitably, Muhoro was arrested. He was convicted and jailed for two months. Upon release, he went back to the marikiti where Grol found him lurking about and looking for something to eat. The priest took him to a village in the Murang'a area, an hour's drive from Nairobi, in the hope that the boy would unwind and become involved in productive work there. But instead, Muhoro ran away, back to the city.

Grol found him again and took him to the reception centre, which at that time was still situated in Westlands. A month later, the boy ran away yet again.

Then one day, Muhoro thought: "If I continue like this, I'll end up a very sad person." He returned to Westlands of his own accord and stayed there for two years. He then went to Undugu's home in Eastleigh, enrolled at one of the schools and completed the three-year course in basic education.

"Now I can make three-piece suites — you know, sofas and armchairs — and stools, tables, beds, doors and windows, all by myself," he says proudly.

Muhoro earns Ksh600 (US$37.50) a month as an apprentice. Undugu gives him another Ksh350 (US$22) to help meet the costs of his food and accommodation. He considers these sums to be a "lot of money", no doubt because they are the largest he has ever handled: "I can now stand on my own two feet and cope with other financial problems," he says.

Muhoro is also motivated by the example of some of

'I can now stand on my own two feet and cope with other financial problems.'

the boys with whom he received his training. "Many of them are now big people," he says. "They have property and have saved up much money." As far as George Muhoro is concerned, Undugu has meant the difference between leading a useful, honest life and a career of petty crime marked by insecurity and periodic

AGAINST ALL ODDS

At Undugu the boys learn a range of skills.

imprisonment. He is aware of the contrast between his life and that of his friends who have stayed on the streets. The latter "continue to steal and risk being locked up in jail. At best they live as scavengers," he says.

Muhoro's ambition is to become a successful carpenter. He hopes that, once he has bought some tools, Undugu will help him to get a loan from the bank to set up his own business. He is determined and says that, without hard work, you can't achieve anything. Because he has been down and out and knows the difference between his old way of life and his present prospects, Muhoro is able to commment on why some boys prefer street life to the chance of a better future with Undugu.

"In the streets, there is no discipline. You think you can do what you like, but you can't really. The police catch you sooner or later. Here you have to control your feelings, you have to have some discipline," he says. "But it's worth it, because eventually you really can lead your own life. "

A mix of aspirations

Christopher "Kazee" Kelly is 17 years old but looks only about 13. He is the fourth in a family of six children and appears keen about what Undugu is doing for him. "I have a bed, water, soap, food and clothing," he says. All he has to do in return is help with the house chores which include washing dishes and sweeping floors. He hopes to get into an Undugu school, and he adds: "I want to become a driver."

Kennedy Mwaura is 13 and has two brothers who are also being cared for by Undugu. They left their original home, close to Nairobi, when their mother died and there was no one reliable to look after them. Mwaura's housefather, John Muiruri, says that Kennedy is always at the top of his class and aspires to be an engineer.

Samuel Nabutanyi is probably the only non-Kenyan in Undugu's care. He fled from Uganda with his father during Idi Amin's reign of terror. "I want to be a doctor," he says. Meanwhile, he is keen to be a member of the Undugu beat band.

David Mutua, aged 15, left home because of the endless tensions

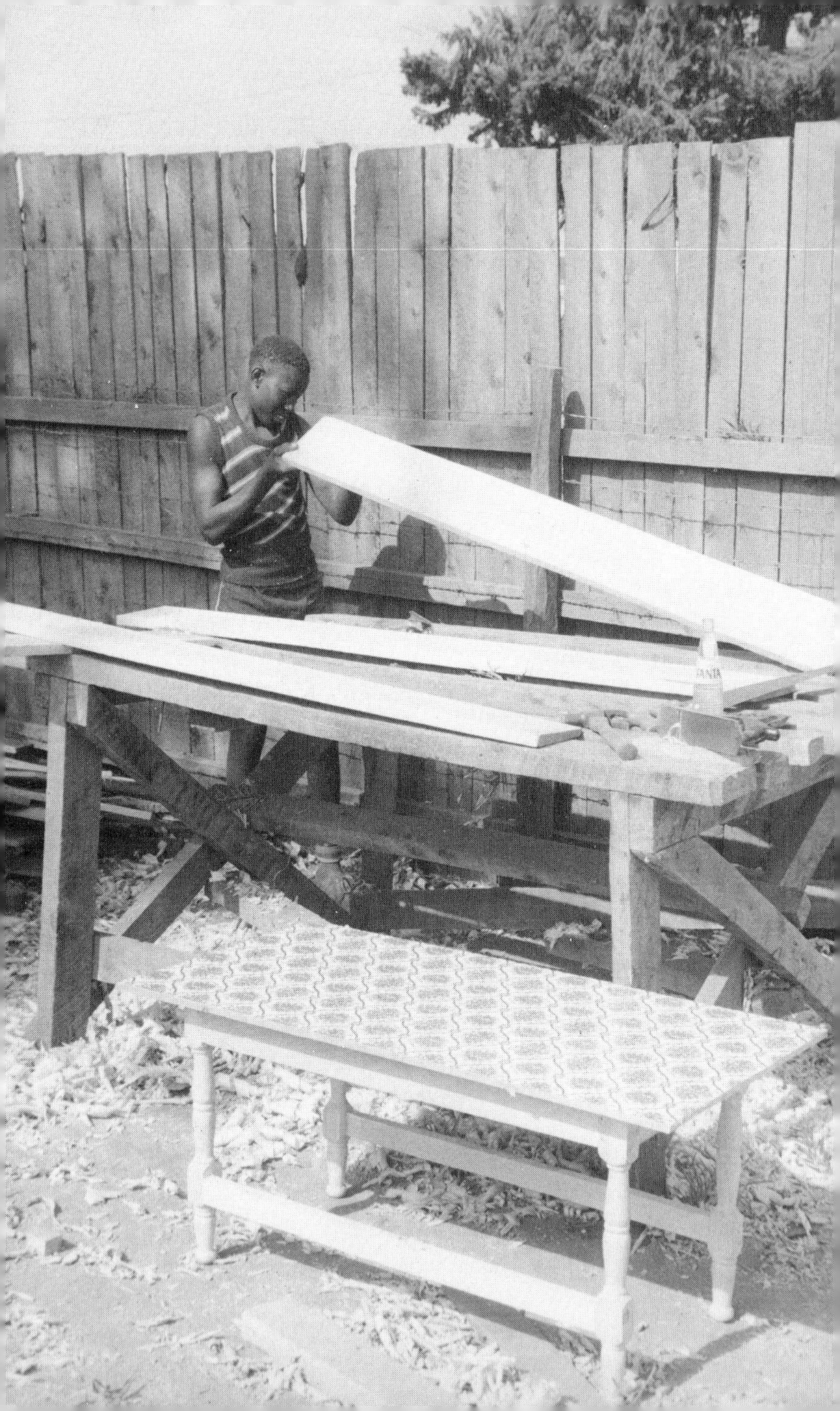

KENYA: The parking boys of Nairobi

and rows there. He refuses to say what his mother does, replying simply: "I can't tell you." He is technically minded, likes doing things with his hands and has a transistor radio at his bedside which he has put together himself.

David Kamau wants to be a carpenter, and Martin Ndung'u was brought to Undugu by Grol and is unusual in his ambition to become a farmer.

The aspirations expressed by the boys show that Undugu is succeeding, at least with some of them, not only in keeping alive a desire to improve themselves, but also the will to work to make their dreams come true.

Blazing a trail for others

"Undugu is really far ahead of the other NGOs in Kenya," says a liaison officer with an organisation which has funded a number of the society's projects. "In a way that sets it apart from the others, Undugu is able, and always willing, to look critically at what it is doing and the effect it is having on the larger community."

Some would say, however, that this tendency to look inwards, to review and continually redesign projects, is Undugu's Achilles heel. It has resulted in a whole range of experimental projects with poor people, to such an extent that some critics believe it is in danger of spreading itself too thinly to make any lasting impact in any one place.

However, through the lessons learnt from its many projects, the society has begun to redefine its programmes — not as ends in themselves, but as pilot projects which other groups in the wider community may adopt as they see fit. The mistakes it has made in the past need not be repeated by other organisations dealing with the problems of slum dwellers. They can learn from the way Undugu deals with children in the context of their families and poverty-stricken background.

And, of course, there is living proof that even the bleakest outlook can be made bright — the former sidewalk hustlers and thieves who are now well on their way to running their own businesses.

INDIA

NO LONGER NEED THEY ABANDON HOME

USHA RAI

INDIA:
No longer need they abandon home

USHA RAI

"Bhal", which means "forehead" in Gujarati, is a vast, desolate wasteland, uninterrupted by vegetation as far as the eye can see. Endless stretches of salt-covered earth glisten in the sun like marble dust, making the air shimmer with mirages in every direction.

Here, some 6 kilometres (3.75miles) from the crescent-shaped Gulf of Khambat in India's Gujarat state, lies the remote district of Dhanduka, once famous for its rich and abundant cotton crop.

The mangroves and jungles of the not-so-distant past are now but a memory, a grim reminder of the swift and total destruction of the environment through over-exploitation. Camel caravans moving southwards from the deserts of Rajasthan and the Raan of Kutch are believed to have destroyed the landscape by eating the mangroves and other vegetation, slowly but surely stripping the land, leaving the coastline naked and exposed to the sea.

For decades now, the sea water has been gushing in at high tide, smothering all traces of the scant vegetation under its trails of salt. The resulting salinity has rendered the land impossible to cultivate, forcing some 70% of the villagers to migrate for the best part of the year in search of drinking water, thereby breaking down the family structure and threatening the very heart of the community.

Serious health epidemics have also erupted as a result of the scarcity of fresh water: dysentery, diarrhoea, dehydration, typhoid and cholera are rife.

INDIA: No longer need they abandon home

Dhandhuka Taluka, Gujarat

The villagers' health is further undermined by a poor diet. Pulses, known locally as "dhal", the staple food of the poor in India, requires a great deal of water for cooking and is therefore not eaten in the summer months.

In an area forsaken by the government as incapable of being developed, the villagers have struggled to eke out a living.

But things are changing. And changing fast. The area is being transformed by the courage and tenacity of a small but dedicated self-help group working hand in hand with the villagers. The organisation is "Mahiti" (knowledge); their achievement — a significant breakthrough in restoring a water supply to the region, and with it, the very life of the family and the community.

Mahiti, which is an offshoot of a government organisation, set about talking to the villagers, encouraging them to articulate their views, and formulate ideas for possible solutions. Unlike the government, Mahiti was not convinced that the difficulties were insurmountable; rather that the region represented some of the severest challenges in the field of development that should be tackled.

> *'Things are changing. And changing fast.'*

After a series of discussions with the villagers, it became apparent that the core of the region's problems lay in the scarcity of water. Before any significant development could take place, this had to be resolved. Only then could the population break the cycle of enforced migration and concentrate on efforts to improve the land.

Today, after several years of experiments and mistakes, the rainwater ponds, initiated and constructed by the villagers themselves, are a testimony to what can be achieved by the self-help approach of organisations like Mahiti.

Ineffective water programmes

Although the government has long recognised the severity of the situation, official attempts to solve the water supply problem have been largely ineffective. The 95-kilometre (60-mile) pipeline, carrying drinking water from the Sabarmati River to 33 villages in the district, is beset with functional problems: loss of pressure; insufficient supply of water at source; leakages and breakdowns along the line, and numerous management problems in operating the pumps.

In the sweltering summer heat, water from the pipeline is reduced to a mere trickle, with the worst-hit villages supplied for a total of 20 to 30 minutes at odd hours. In the inevitable scramble for water that results, fights frequently break out.

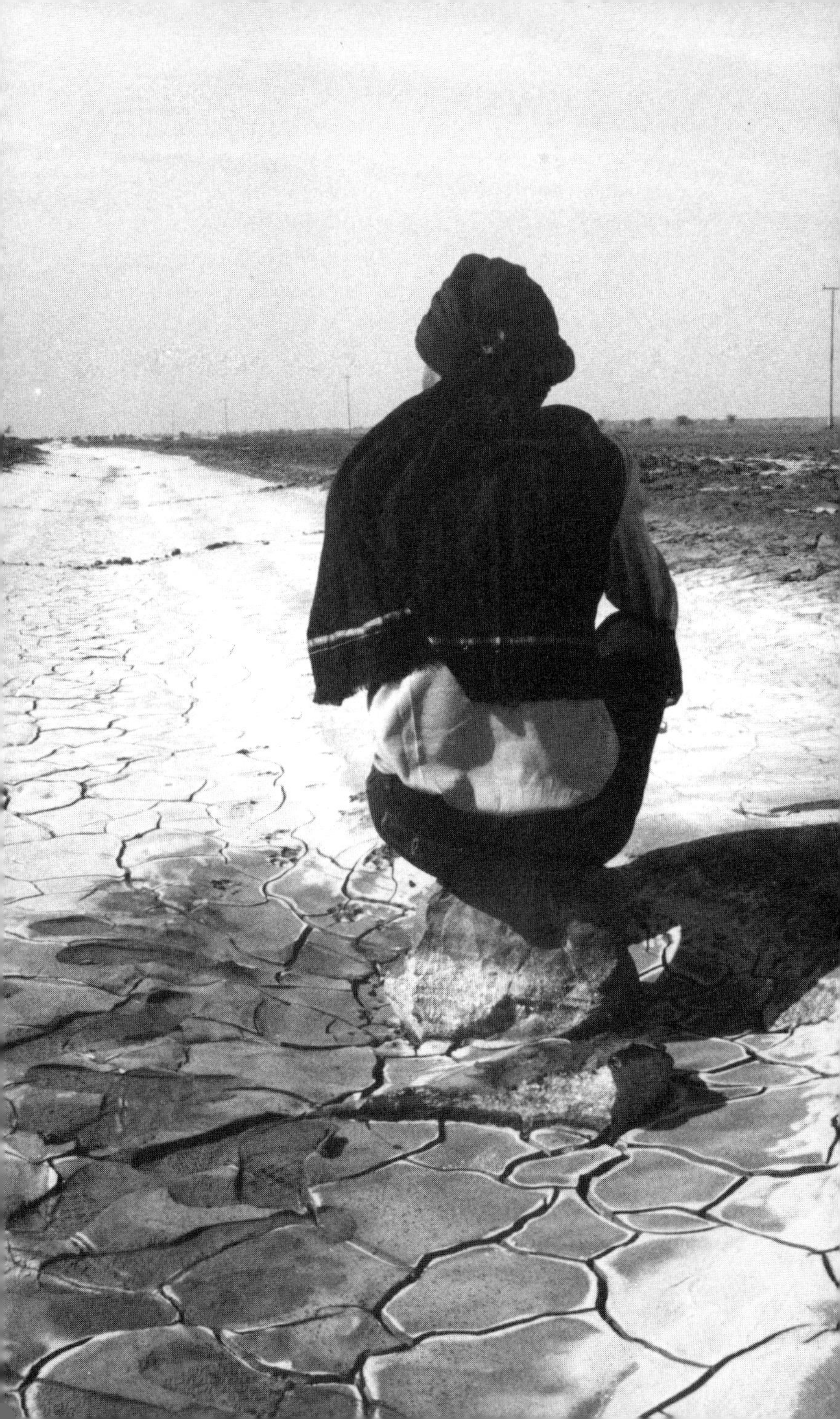

The government's attitude was wholly defeatist. The official line was that, given the magnitude of the problem, any efforts at improvement were bound to end in frustration and disappointment; the villagers, it was said, would do better to migrate elsewhere. So convinced were officials that this was the only viable option, that they did their utmost to dissuade members of Mahiti from breaking away from the parent group to embark on their own efforts.

Mahiti's history

Mahiti became involved with the villagers in a rather roundabout way. In the mid-1970s the state government of Gujarat decided to involve non-governmental organisations (NGOs) in the process of development planning; solutions, it said, should not only comprise the ideas of people at the top, but also those whose lives would ultimately be affected.

Planning responsibility for the remote Dhandhuka areas of Ahmedabad district was given to the Ahmedabad Study Action Group (ASAG). By 1980 the group had outlined the problems of the district and worked out a strategy for its development.

ASAG's planning unit identified the Bhal region as the most backward and underdeveloped part of the "taluka" (subdivision of the district) and was keen to take on the challenge of attacking the problems.

However, neither its own parent group, ASAG, nor the state government was willing to allow the planning unit to go ahead and tackle the problems identified. ASAG's argument was that the villages were too far away from Ahmedabad — between 150 and 160 kilometres (94-100 miles) — and since there was no public transport to the area, it would be extremely difficult to commute there.

But the members of the planning unit persisted. The Bhal region represented an enormous challenge which they were not prepared to ignore.

The planning unit finally broke away from ASAG in 1980 and started Mahiti a year later. It was to be an agency to help people articulate their problems and ideas in a clear and forceful way; an

INDIA: No longer need they abandon home

Villagers are forced to migrate in search of drinking water, breaking down family structures.

organisation founded on the belief that, given the opportunity, people can often identify the solution that is most workable within their own context.

"Our organisation is only a catalyst," says Nafisa Barot, Mahiti's dynamic executive trustee. "We supply information and build the bridges of communication that haven't been built before. Mahiti will not run the project — it will only mobilise and motivate the people to work for themselves. Five out of nine members of Mahiti are actually villagers."

Long and arduous process

In this spirit, Mahiti set to work. The process has been long and arduous.

Land salinity has been difficult to overcome. The groundwater table has a prohibitive saline content of 50,000 parts per million (ppm), in comparison with 35,000 ppm in sea water. Rainfall is erratic, ranging from 30 to 160 centimetres (12 to 63 inches), with 65 centimetres (26 inches) in normal years.

This semi-arid area is afflicted by both droughts and floods with one ordeal sometimes following the other in quick succession.

Since 1982, the region has been repeatedly hit by drought. Yet water-logging has also been a frequent occurrence. In a given year, the drought tends to last until September, and is then broken by a few heavy downpours which result in severe flooding.

This cycle is aggravated by both the flat terrain which lacks vegetation to absorb excess water and the non-porous quality of the black clayey soil.

Wind speeds of up to 32 kilometres (20 miles) per hour resulting in severe wind erosion, only add to the list of problems.

As if these natural conditions were not bad enough, the area is also fraught with socio-economic problems. The people in the villages involved — Zhanki (population 600), Rajpur (800), Mahadevpura (1,000), Khun (1,200), Rahatalav (1,500), Bhangadh (2,000) and Mingalpur (3,000) — are Kohli Patels, regarded as a backward caste in India's social stratification system.

Both the local economy and the people are controlled by the "darbars", the feudal landlords of the past who have evolved into today's money-lenders.

A desolate scenario

Government staff, whether teachers, health workers or "gram sevak" (village workers paid by the local administration), find it difficult to visit these villages, let alone live in them.

When water is hard to find, the villagers' only assets — their cows and bullocks — also face extinction. Given the shortage of water, there is no fodder either. It is not uncommon for families to give whatever there is to drink to their animals, which still often die soon after. Almost every village has a section where the carcasses of the dead cattle are thrown.

The villagers' anguish is immeasurable when their cattle die because the animals are usually their only source of milk and sustenance in summer.

One of Mahiti's first exploratory ventures was to try and tap solar

INDIA: No longer need they abandon home

power to distil saline water into drinking water. After several field tests, however, this was abandoned as unsuitable for the region and too expensive.

Mahiti also tried to collect rainwater running off the sloping roofs of houses, using funnels and positioning pipes into cement tanks. This technique was tested at the organisation's experimental centre, known as the People's Learning Centre, situated between the villages of Khun and Rahatalav.

In individual homes in the arid parts of Rajasthan, a year's supply of water is collected and stored in this way. At the Mahiti Centre, 20,000 litres (4,350 gallons) of rainwater can be stored in a cement tank built at a cost of Rupees 18,000 (US$1,400). Tin sheets cover the tank to prevent evaporation.

Although large volumes of water can be accumulated in this way, the initial costs of the tank are too high for the villagers to afford.

Since large loans and grants are difficult to come by, Mahiti has abandoned this scheme, too, until further experimentation allows costs to be reduced.

Mahiti experiments to collect rainwater.

The one desalinisation scheme which Mahiti has tried and which has proved truly successful is a process which involves filtering water through a membrane.

Water experts in India have long believed that there are streams or rivers flowing well below the saline water table. In 1982 Mahiti sank a borewell and hit a fountain of hot water at 300 metres (1,000 feet). Although the water turned out to be brackish, its salt content was only 5,000 ppm — a tenth of the sub-soil water.

Mahiti then conducted tests which showed that this method of collecting drinking water was not only workable, but purification could prove cost-effective.

Reducing health hazards

The process is a simple one: saline water is pumped through a cylinder containing a membrane which filters out the salt. This process also rids the water of organisms and therefore reduces many of the hazards which threaten health.

The Gram Vikas Samiti, an NGO based in Ahmedabad, bought and installed such a unit at Dholera, the nearest city to the seven coastal villages with which Mahiti was involved. The unit was given to the "zilla parishad" (local administration) to run.

All the investigations and hard work to find a reliable and abundant source of drinking water came to naught however, because the unit was locked up and not used. The individual responsible for operating it kept disappearing for days on end and the administration seemed incapable of getting it working. Rumours began to spread that harmful drugs had been mixed into the water. This situation lasted for no less than five years and it was only in August 1987 that the unit was handed over to Mahiti to operate.

At present, Mahiti is trying to raise funds to run it. Costs, including wages and depreciation, work out at one or two paise per litre (less than one-tenth of one US cent per litre). The method makes it possible to desalinise 800 litres (175 gallons) an hour.

Moujibhai, a Mahiti worker who lives at Khun village, and Tejinder Bhogal, a rural management graduate working with

INDIA: No longer need they abandon home

Villagers gather at the Mahiti centre for the 'Bhal' region.

Mahiti, are both convinced that the scheme is practical and cost-effective: "It is better than bringing water in by tankers from a distance of 70 kilometres (45 miles)," they say. "It costs Rs400 (US$30) to bring one tanker to this taluka, carrying 9,000 litres (1,960 gallons)."

The new method, Mahiti claims, could produce 16,000 litres (3,480 gallons) of drinkable water at a cost of US$15 without dependence on external help. The scheme could be replicated wherever necessary, without all the problems associated with buying tankers of water from Dholera.

What then is holding the project back?

While no one makes any direct accusations, the villagers lament that "Dholera is a den of corruption", implying that it is no accident that the water-purifying unit has not been able to function.

Rainwater catchment ponds — the people's idea

Meanwhile, Mahiti seems to have hit the jackpot with an idea originated by the people themselves: the construction of eight rainwater catchment ponds lined with plastic film.

A pond is now located in every village; Mingalpur, with the largest population, has two.

Villagers travelling to the town of Surat for work had seen the way the canals there were lined to prevent loss of water through seepage. They suggested that the same method be used, and that the plastic sheeting be backed up by a layer of pitch-tar on the pond wall.

The plastic lining would not only prevent seepage, but would act as a barrier to salt. The villagers also suggested that each pond should have a proper inlet for water, be deeper, and large enough to meet the needs of all the people and cattle in the village.

Mahiti tested the idea and consulted outside engineers about ways to build the ponds and make the plastic totally non-porous. As the ponds are in areas of natural depression, the rainwater flows into them effortlessly.

Experiments were carried out at the Mahiti Centre with plastic film provided by the Indian Petrochemicals Corporation Limited (IPCL). The results spurred the villagers at Rahatalav to build a similar pond. It took two years and was completed in 1985.

So enthusiastic were the people about what seemed to them their only hope of drinking water, that they worked for two months for no wages at all. The plastic film was again supplied by IPCL free of charge.

The official go-ahead

Three other villages — Khun, Mingalpur and Mahadevpura — were quick to follow suit. By this time the Gujarat Water Supply and Sewage Board (GWSSB) was also convinced of the need for such projects and agreed to supervise their implementation. It was agreed that the government's National Rural Employment Programme would pay the wages of the villagers engaged in excavation work.

GWSSB's only conditions for helping were that the water be

INDIA: No longer need they abandon home

Supplies of precious drinking water have halted enforced migration .

filtered to make it hygienic, and that the point of access should be outside the pond itself. This would ensure that the water in the pond remained clean. Although the villagers agreed to these conditions, work kept being delayed so that excavation in all three villages had still not been completed by the time the rains came. Khun had done the most, completing about 80% of the work.

Since Rahatalav was the only village with a pond that had accumulated drinking water, people and cattle from surrounding villages descended on this abundant supply.

Community guards were unable to check the stampede, with the result that the mud packs holding down the lining were broken and the lining itself was torn in several places.

Important lessons learnt

Neither the villagers nor Mahiti were disheartened, however. In fact, the disruption taught them an important lesson. Instead of mud packs, they decided to secure the plastic lining with proper brickwork.

Rahatalav has since renovated its pond. Mingalpur decided it would build a second one, and Rajpur, Zhanki and Bhangadh all applied for drinking-water facilities.

Unfortunately, the GWSSB chairman was transferred and the board then lost interest in the project.

The "mahila mandals" (women's groups) which had been mobilised by Mahiti were, however, determined to see the projects completed. They took the initiative and met with several government officials whom they convinced that the ponds were vitally important.

> *'Women accepted the moral responsibility of completing the ponds.'*

In November/December 1986 the secretary and joint secretary to the Ministry of Rural Development visited Rahatalav and conferred with the women. The women explained why several thousand people from the seven villages found it necessary to migrate every year. They made it clear that, if the government

INDIA: No longer need they abandon home

supported the pond-building projects, the majority would stay put, initially to help construct the ponds for wages on a daily basis and later because the water would make other activities possible.

What is more, the women accepted the moral responsibility of completing the ponds within an agreed time. The officials were convinced and work restarted in January 1987.

Putting up the money

Funds for the excavation work were allocated under the government's National Rural Employment Programme. In addition, Council for Advancement of People's Action and Rural

The Mahiti research centre at Rahatalav propagates local plant varieties which can withstand the harsh rural environment.

Technology (CAPART), a government organisation, provided Rs3.5 million (US$270,000) for the plastic lining for the ponds.

So dedicated were the villagers that all eight ponds were ready before the monsoons of 1987.

The smallest pond is at Zhanki, it measures 86 x 56 metres (284 x 185 feet) at the top and 74 x 44 metres (244 x 145 feet) at the base. Like all the other ponds, it is 2.7 metres (9 feet) deep.

Migration pattern changed

The people and animals at Zhanki need 11,000 cubic metres of water per annum, and their pond can hold 12,000 cubic metres. The capacity of the largest pond, at Bhangadh, is 28,800 cubic metres. Each pond has an inlet and a pipe that leads the water to a treatment plant where it is filtered. It then flows into a tank which is fitted with a handpump to draw out the water. Another outlet pipe takes water to a trough which the animals drink from. The natural gradient of the land is used at all points to regulate the flow of water.

Although the villagers were ready with their ponds, for the fifth consecutive year the monsoons failed. Only at Rahatalav and at the Mahiti Centre was there any significant rainfall in 1987. The other ponds remained bone dry.

And yet about 80% of the villagers chose not to migrate. This refusal to leave their homes marked a psychological breakthrough. It indicated that the people had confidence in the projects which they, together with Mahiti, had conceived and created.

> *'About 80% of the villagers chose not to migrate.'*

The attitude of the Ministry of Rural Development has also been transformed by the villagers' tenacity. The ministry is now convinced that lined ponds are a workable way to collect and store water in the saline coastal areas of Gujarat and in those parts of Rajasthan where water is scarce.

Geologists of MS University at Baroda believe this technique could also be used to collect run-off water in the hills. But the true effectiveness of the lined ponds in the Bhal region will only be known when they have been able to store water for a period of at least two years.

A major problem at Rahatalav in 1987 was checking the evaporation from the large exposed surface of the pond. The rate at which water evaporates is such that the pond is likely to lose some 40% of its contents over a year.

Unnerved by this possibility, Mahiti's volunteers desperately tried to cover the pond with plastic sheets — which were blown about by the strong winds.

As far as community involvement is concerned, however, the projects have been an undoubted success. Women have played a leading role at every stage and have become a strong, cohesive force in the region. They have supervised construction and ensured that the workers were not cheated of their wages; cement quality was closely monitored to ensure that it was not diluted. At the Rahatalav pond, they ensure that there is no panic drinking, and that the water remains clean.

Women who for years had been suppressed and remained in the background have suddenly become vocal, assertive, and ready to meet their responsibilities.

Tree-planting

Although Mahiti's social forestry programme — tree-planting by the community — started in 1982, the arid landscape has meant that it is still very much at the embryonic stage.

Barren and desolate though it is, land is the only resource of the people in Bhal region. Some families own as much as 50 hectares (125 acres) but lack the means to develop their holdings. Others have neither land nor any visible means of support, having mortgaged their plots to money-lenders in five consecutive years of drought.

But they can acquire wasteland from the government for purposes of social forestry, which has been given high priority for environmental reasons. Villagers feel that trees are vital for improving the productivity of the land, for checking wind and sea erosion, and for trapping the excess rainwater which, in the absence of trees, causes flash floods.

Social forestry also provides work for people on the brink of destitution. It is a programme around which villagers can be organised in a way that helps them to help themselves.

Most of the social forestry pilot projects are tried out at the Mahiti Centre on the 20 hectares (50 acres) of land leased to this NGO.

> *'Trees are vital for improving the productivity of the land, and for checking wind and sea erosion and flash flooding.'*

By talking to the villagers, Mahiti personnel have discovered that *Salvadora piludi* and *Prosopis julliflora,* the latter locally known as "ganda bawla" were plants indigenous to the region. Both these trees also have economic value.

The *Salvadora* produces berries and fruit. A non-edible oil is extracted from the berries and used by the soap and cosmetics industry. The residue is used as fertiliser in the paddy and tobacco fields. The fruit is edible and is often exchanged for wheat.

The ganda bawla tree grows equally well either in rocky terrain or in sandy soil. Its branches can be used as fuelwood, its pods as cattle feed, its leaves and bark have medicinal properties, and charcoal can be produced from its trunk.

Mahiti has worked out various techniques with the villagers for growing the trees with minimum amounts of water and using everything available. Workers have found that trench cultivation maximises the amount of water that can be retained and provides channels for draining it when flooding occurs.

Plantations of *Salvadora* and *Prosopis julliflora* have been started at Khun and Rahalatav — about 25 hectares (63 acres) in each village. Mingalpur, Mahadevpura, Zhanki and Rajpur have also embarked on this tree-planting scheme, but on a smaller scale because they have found it difficult to get loans or financial aid.

After unsuccessful attempts at gaining assistance from banks and money-lenders for the social forestry projects, Mahiti turned to the National Wasteland Development Board (NWDB), which provided funds to launch two large nurseries — one of them with 120,000 saplings.

Exploiting the local trees

Seventy one-hectare plantations of *Salvadora* and *Prosopis* were also started with NWDB assistance in 1987, at Khun, Rahatalav, Mahadevpura and Zhanki. On each hectare, 840 *Salvadora* and 400 *Prosopis* saplings are grown, the latter ringing the *Salvadora*. The plantations are protected by fencing made from dried thorny *Prosopis*.

It takes three to four years for the *Salvadora* to start bearing fruit and become an economic asset. Three kilos of oil can be extracted from 20 kilograms of berries, each kilo of oil selling for Rs20 (US$1.50). In 1987, it was the women of Mingalpur who did the oil-extracting work in the village.

The *Prosopis* can be pruned five years after planting and its branches used as fuel wood. Thereafter, cuttings can be made at four-year intervals.

Although some of the villages, such as Mingalpur and Rahatalav, have successfully grown *Salvadora* and made some money from selling its berries, by and large Mahiti's social forestry programme is still only beginning.

Changed attitudes

Villagers are becoming aware of the possibilities offered by the trees: more and more of them are applying for plots of government wasteland and starting their own *Salvadora* and *Prosopis* plantations.

The most evident change is in the attitudes of the villagers themselves. Their sense of helplessness has slowly dissipated, and has been replaced by a belief in their own ability to act and change things for the better.

Yasodha, of Bhangadh village, exemplifies the new awareness and the awakening of the people to their own power. She has grown a *Salvadora* tree in the little courtyard of her house and sells about 60 kilograms of berries a year for Rs100 (US$8). And as a member of the women's group, she has collected 18,000 kilograms of berries from the three villages and undertaken to sell them herself.

Yasodha says that Bhangadh will soon have its plantation of *Salvadora* and that the trees will be grown along with "jowar" (millet): "The leaves of the *Salvadora* will improve the soil so that we can then grow grass and fodder crops for our cattle," she says.

It is at the Mahiti Centre, however, that one is best able to visualise the outcome of the social forestry programme and to follow the lines of research being pursued.

Mahiti has identified and experimented with several species of trees capable of thriving in the Bhal region. They are truly tough and able to withstand high levels of salt, heavy soils, drought, water-logging and grazing animals.

Several of the plants are thorny and therefore cannot be grazed by cattle. The Tamarix is a good fuel tree and serves well as a windbreak. *Derris indica* yields fruit from which oil can be extracted for the soap industry. What is more, animals don't like it. The *Prosopis cineraria* grows around ponds and water holes in soil that isn't too saline. Cattle eat its leaves and it is a good fuelwood tree.

A fruitful future

The people at Khun proudly showed me the village's first pomegranate tree which has inspired others to follow suit. Its first crop of 60 pomegranates was followed by considerable jubilation as it pointed the way to better days ahead.

The villagers are also experimenting with "neem" (*Azadirachta indica*), which has medicinal properties and the ability to purify air, and with the "goras amli" fruit tree (*Pithecollobium dulce*) too.

With a few hundred head of cattle dying every year in the drought conditions, fodder crops are badly needed. The people at Khun therefore plan to grow fodder on a 64-hectare (160-acre) plot on the other side of the creek where the grazing animals cannot get to it. They intend to replant the mangroves as well.

Moujibhai, a Mahiti worker who lives at Khun, says the "yuva mandal" (youth organisation) will be in charge of fodder cultivation and responsible for protecting the coastal zone. The idea is that two or three members of the youth wing will live on the coast to guard the mangroves and fodder crops against marauding people and cattle.

Mahiti's long-term hope is to re-establish the mangroves that once protected this stretch of the Gujarat coastline. To make this possible, the people will be shown how to build a tidal embankment with stones to act as the front line of defence against sea erosion.

'Mahiti's long-term hope is to re-establish the mangroves that once protected this stretch of the Gujurat coastline.'

Freedom from debt

Women's groups were mobilised by Mahiti at Mingalpur, Bhangadh and Mahadevpura in 1984, and at Khun a youth group is very active. It is these people who discuss local problems with the villagers, help them to find solutions and carry out programmes of action.

"Once the people think clearly about the issues that affect them and become involved in the development process, economic benefits are bound to follow in which they will share," says a young Mahiti enthusiast.

Just how much things have changed since Mahiti adopted these seven villages is illustrated by the experience of Bhangadh, where five consecutive years of drought have driven the villagers into the clutches of the money-lenders to whom they have mortgaged their land. Many of the villagers have run away to the cities because they could no longer face interest rates of between 12% and 20%. The more desperate the villagers, the higher the interest rate. And the rate then doubles with each succeeding year.

Yet in Bhangadh the women have started a savings scheme. Their groups meet twice a month and the members chip in whatever

Cattle play a major part in people's lives. Cattle camps protect animals from starvation, and reduce the vulnerability of the people to money-lenders.

they can afford, even if it's only a rupee or two (Rs13 = US$1), to a village fund.

Whenever the women earn a bit of money, either by doing contract labour or by selling the salvador berries, they deposit part of their earnings into the fund.

Each of the three groups has accumulated Rs5,000 (US$385) and is able to make loans of between Rs50 and Rs100 (US$4 to US$8) to their neighbours.

"We no longer have to run to the money-lenders for small amounts," says Hira.

It was also the women's groups, in association with Mahiti, which in 1986 organised a cattle camp to save the starving animals. This meant that manure could also be collected at one point in the village and used to fertilise the land.

A similar cattle camp was organised in 1987. Using money from a private trust supplemented with government funds, the women supplied drinking water and fodder to 2,000 head of cattle from the seven villages for 45 days. Survival of their cattle has a multiplier effect on the people, and one important consequence is that their vulnerability to exploitation by the darbars — the money-lenders — has been greatly reduced. The exercise was repeated in 1988.

> *'One important consequence is that the villagers' vulnerability to the 'darbars' — money-lenders — has been greatly reduced.'*

Mahiti's funding

In 1987 Mahiti received a grant of Rs476,000 (US$37,000) from the Aga Khan Foundation, Rs340,000 (US$26,000) from Oxfam and US$27,000 from the Holden India Fund.

CAPART has given Rs1.8 million (US$140,000) for construction of the eight lined ponds, and the Khadi Village Industries Commission has provided a loan of Rs90,000 (US$7,000) to the women's groups to set them up as salvadora berry traders.

"Mahiti will need external funding for another three or four years," says executive trustee Nafisa Barot.

But by then the charcoal industry and the salvadora-oil extracting business should be in full swing. "We will then have a fodder plantation at our centre and be fully independent," Nafisa adds. And, she argues, the teams at the village level will be strong enough to meet the people's needs, so the improvements made so far are clearly sustainable.

Nafisa and her colleagues are optimists. Were it not for their drive and dedication, the region's prospects would not have changed so much for the better. Together with the villagers, Mahiti is involved in a programme to rescue the environment from its salt-laden desolation.

Being a cynical journalist, however, I see many more years of struggle ahead for Mahiti — primarily against bureaucracy and the exploitative society. But at least someone has risen to the challenge with such courage and persistence.

For the first time in many decades, some hope exists in the otherwise desolate Bhal region. For the first time, the people there see no reason to abandon their homes.

KENYA

THE WATER THAT
BRINGS NEW LIFE

WINNIE OGANA

KENYA: The water that brings new life

WINNIE OGANA

With her feet on the cement rim of the gaping water well, the Kenyan girl balances herself precariously as she lowers a jerrycan at the end of a rope to the water some 10 metres (33 feet) below.

Seconds later, the can hits the water with a splash. The girl tugs at the rope several times to get the water flowing into the can, and after a while begins to pull her heavy cargo of 20 litres (4 gallons) up to the surface.

She seems unaware of the danger of her feet slipping as she hauls up her load of water, and the danger of tumbling to her death down the dark pit. She is more concerned about not letting any of the water spill from the can as it sways to and fro on its way up the well. The girl is typical of many other females in Kenya's coastal villages of the Kwale district who risk their lives each time they go to draw water from the well.

The villagers have seen women doing this chore so often over the years that they no longer perceive the danger involved. To them, balancing above a deep well is simply a part of everyday life. But visitors to the village become tense as they watch the women performing the dangerous and laborious exercise.

According to the people in the area, each family in a village risks the life of one of its members in this way about eight times a day. This is because the average family has eight members, each requiring one canful of water a day.

KENYA: The water that brings new life

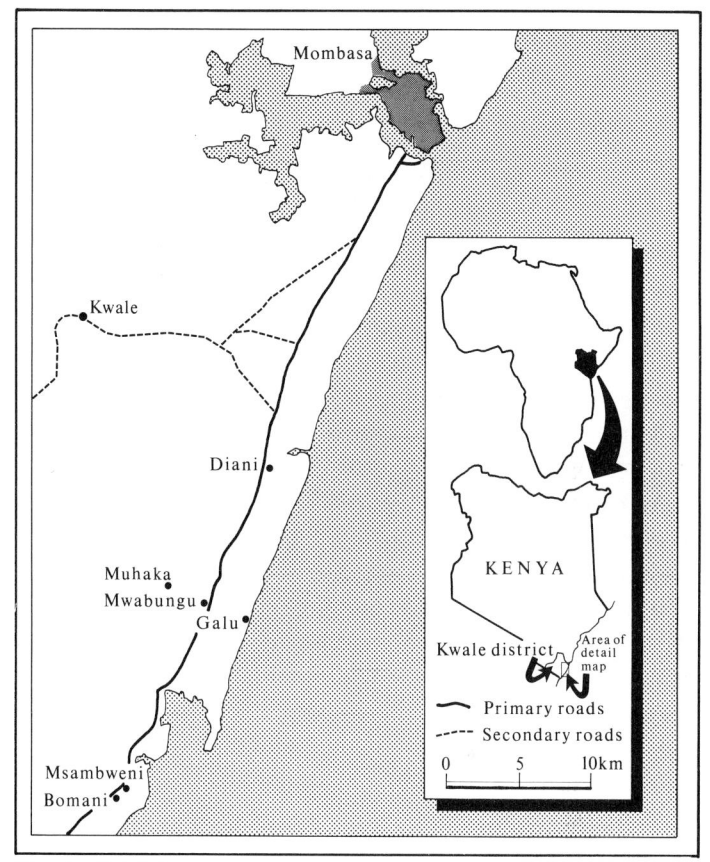

Kwale district

Moreover, some of the wells in the area are 100 metres deep, increasing the danger of any fall and making the work of pulling up the water even more exhausting.

The wells are not even nearby. The village women trudge an average of 3 kilometres (nearly 2 miles) to the nearest source of water, and the same distance back with their precious, but heavy, containers. And when those sources dry up, which happens frequently, they have to walk further, spending more time in their quest for water.

With so much time and effort involved in getting water, it isn't surprising that the women would prefer to secure their supplies in a way that is not so tiring.

It's better to buy water

Those who can afford to, like Mariamu Hassan, buy their water from a kiosk. Not only does this do away with all the walking and carrying, but the water is cleaner, too. The water piped to the kiosk doesn't have bits of grass in it and other impurities visible to the eye, as is the case with the well water.

Mariamu is in her fifties. She says she would rather pay Kenya shillings 10 (63UScents) per drum of water every day than go through the grinding slog of fetching the water herself from either of the two sources. As far as she is concerned, the river is much too far away. But the other source, although located in a nearby school compound, is a borehole whose cement sides have cracked, making it difficult to draw the water.

Unfortunately, Mariamu has recently had no choice but to go with her container to the school compound because the owner of the water kiosk has again not paid his monthly bill on time and his supply has been cut off by the Water Ministry.

A pilot water programme

In order to ease the water problem, a pilot programme has been under way in the Kwale district of Kenya's Coast province.

Known as the Kwale Water and Sanitation Project, the programme includes the drilling of about 100 boreholes, covering up "traditional" (and dangerous) village wells, and installing handpumps in the Diani and Msambweni locations immediately to the south of the coastal town of Mombasa. These locations each comprise a number of villages, which amount to a rural sprawl.

The aim is to provide safe drinking water in a less arduous way, and basic sanitation. The project is being run by an NGO called the Kenyan Water for Health Organisation (KWAHO).

KWAHO's history goes back to the UN Women's Conference that was held in Mexico in 1975, which set up a voluntary fund for women's projects. The next year, several Kenyan NGOs got together with the United Nations Children's Fund (UNICEF) to set

KENYA: The water that brings new life

Women are no longer forced to risk their lives when drawing water from deep wells.

up a water-for-health project to take advantage of the women's fund in a way that would benefit Kenyans, especially the women.

The purpose of that initial water-for-health project was to support the Kenyan Government's attempts to bring safe water to all its people by the year 2000 and thereby improve the quality of their lives.

The name of the organisation has since changed from the UNICEF/NGO Water for Health Project to KWAHO, but the goals are the same.

In most of Africa, fetching water is perceived as women's work. Right from the start the Kenyan citizens' groups decided to focus on small community-based water projects in which women would take part as planners and implementers and be involved in maintenance, too.

Since its inception, the water programme has supported more than 100 water-related projects to help Kenyan women.

Much of Kenya is either arid or semi-arid. And, again in common with other Third World countries, Kenya faces serious difficulties in trying to keep up with the need for safe and ample supplies of water for its rapidly growing population.

At independence in 1963, Kenya's population was about 7 million, but today it is estimated at 22 million. The population growth rate, at 4.1% a year, is believed to be the highest in the world. Unless the rate of growth falls substantially, the population is likely to double within about 15 years.

Most Kenyans live on 40% of the land, of which only 14% is arable. The rest of the people try to eke out a living in areas where rainfall is sparse and unreliable, even at the best of times. They all need water, a vital factor in any kind of development.

Water is life

"Water is life," says Rose Maluma, a KWAHO programme officer. "Almost everything revolves around it. If the water is not clean, it is bound to undermine the people's health. And if the people aren't strong enough to work, they cannot contribute to development. It's as simple as that."

Kenya's Ministry of Water Development is working hard to provide improved water and sanitation facilities to as many communities as possible. But the ministry acknowledges that this is no easy task. It is concentrating on two aspects of the water problem: low-cost and appropriate technologies, and continuous involvement of local communities in existing, and new, water projects.

Although the ministry is providing engineering and technical solutions for the supply problems, it is not equipped to deal with the social and cultural aspects of the planned water and sanitation systems. And it is precisely in these aspects that KWAHO's activities have proved to be so valuable all over the country.

Experience in Kenya has shown that when the potential beneficiaries of a water-supply project are not themselves involved in running and maintaining the scheme, it is likely to end long before the pump itself breaks down.

So community involvement is another crucial factor in a project's success.

Before the Kwale project was started, two earlier schemes had made the costly mistake of not fully involving the community and spelling out the villagers' role clearly. The first was an international aid project in the 1960s which fitted handpumps to existing wells; it failed because the local people were not committed to it. A similar exercise in the 1970s produced similar results for the same reason.

Rose Maluma: "If water is not clean, it is bound to undermine people's health. And if people aren't strong enough to work, they cannot contribute to development. It's as simple as that."

Strong emphasis on self-help

KWAHO's work always has a strong self-help element. Most of the work, very often, is organised by the local people themselves, especially women's groups, who co-operate with health and water experts from outside and with District Community Development officials.

KWAHO's work has a bearing on the activities of many organisations in Kenya, but its principal partners are: the personnel of the Ministry of Water Development who are in charge of drilling the boreholes and covering over the "traditional" wells; the World Bank, which has been supplying several types of handpumps and providing general technical back-up; the Ministry of Health and the Ministry of Culture and Social Services which have been making available the services of extension workers and administrators without whom, in Kenya, this kind of work cannot progress; and above all, the villagers who form water committees.

The pilot project, in the Diani and Msambweni locations of Kwale district, now under way touches about 50,000 people in 50 villages. The Muslim Digo people of the area are generally occupied in growing cashew nuts, coconuts, mangoes, oranges and tangerines, and some of them live by fishing.

On higher ground are the Christian Kamba people who cultivate maize, beans and other crops. Although the tourist hotels along the coast provide a ready market for fresh produce, both groups of people in the area are poor and enjoy few modern facilities.

The rainfall where they live is moderate, but very seasonal. The streams are dry during most of the year, and although there is ample groundwater, many "traditional" village wells are not deep enough to provide water all year round.

Women have to trek considerable distances to dig for water with their hands, in the beds of dry streams. The water in the streams and wells tends to be foul and unfit for human consumption.

> *'Women have to trek considerable distances to dig for water with their hands, in the beds of dry streams.'*

In the case of these poor people, water only superficially means life. Deeper down, at the level of micro-organisms, it means disease, listlessness and eventual death because of all the impurities.

Mwanaisha Mweropia is a 21-year-old mother of six who lives in Mwabungo village in Kwale district. Until three years ago, she used to make at least seven journeys a day to the nearest borehole, half a kilometre away in neighbouring Mwembeni village, to fetch the seven buckets of water her family needed.

She had to queue afresh for each bucket of water, the rule being that no one could draw a second bucketful if there were other people waiting to draw their supply. And there were always other people waiting. To beat the queue, Mwanaisha would do her best to be at

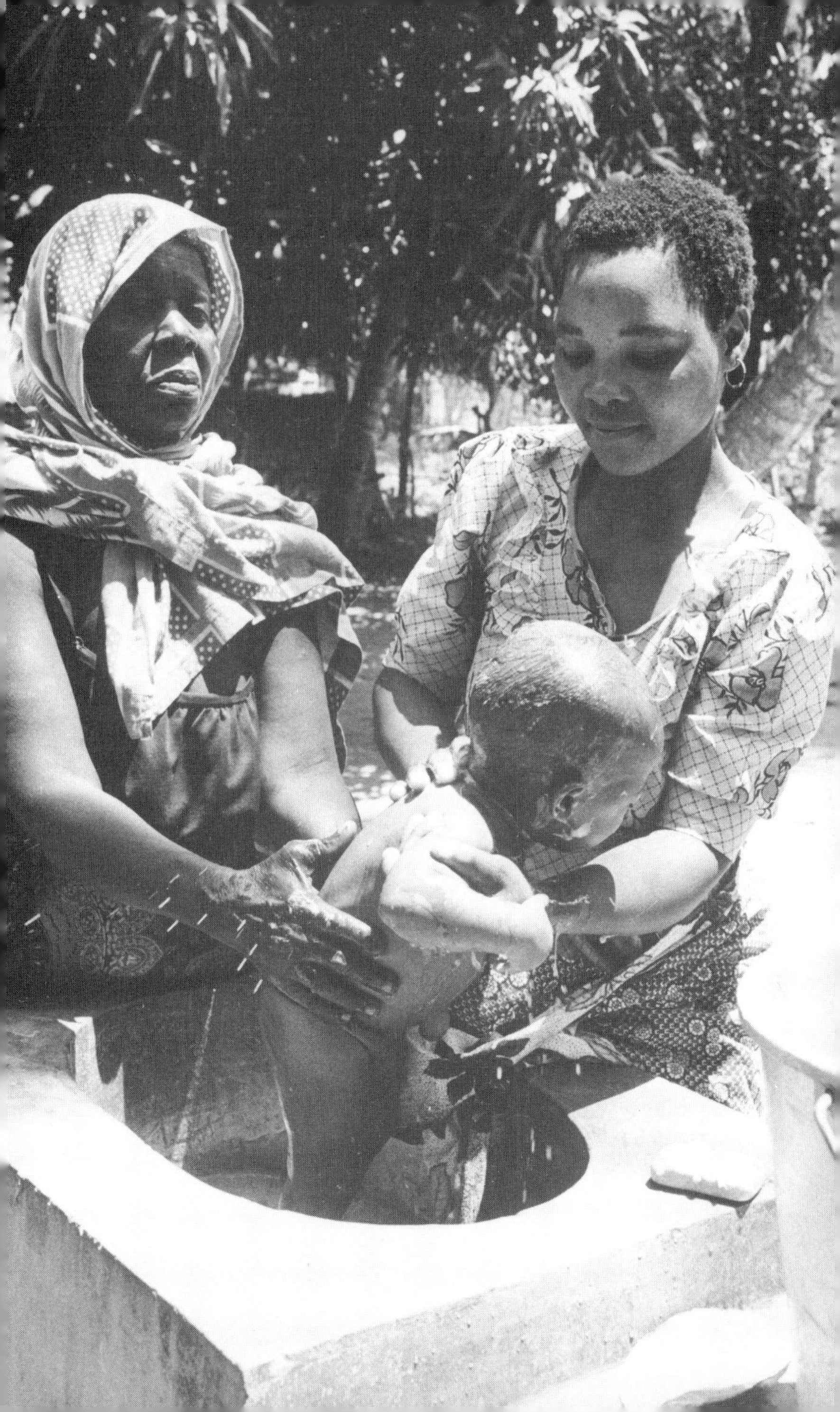

the borehole at the crack of dawn each day. But by the time her family went to bed at night, there would be not a drop left, no sign of all the effort she had put in during the day. And she felt exhausted all the time. Her throat was scraped by a perpetual cough and she kept complaining about chronic chest problems.

A less irksome life ...

Then in 1984, KWAHO installed an Afridev water pump nearby. Mwanaisha says she has found the chore of fetching water much less irksome ever since. She almost enjoys using the handpump with its long handle — it is so much easier than hauling a heavy bucket 10 metres to the surface.

The pump also put an end to the frequent quarrelling and ill-feeling that used to erupt among the village women as they pushed and shoved one another while waiting their turn to draw water from the borehole.

Another reason why Mwanaisha is happy about the pump is that her three daughters will not have to lead the arduous life she has had. She dreams of the day when piped water will be available right in the compound of her home. Meanwhile, as she suckles her 18-month-old baby, she says she is content with the Afridev community pump. What is now only a dream for this mother might well become a reality in the lifetime of her daughters.

... and healthier too

Mwanaisha says that after the pump was installed, her cough gradually disappeared and the pain in her chest stopped troubling her. Indeed, the greatest benefit which the villagers enjoy under the KWAHO programme is improved health.

According to Mwanauba Omar, who works in the project, the incidence of water-related diseases is on the decline. Born in Muhaka village but now married to a Mwabungo villager, she says that, before the Kwale Health and Sanitation Project, bilharzia used to kill about 10 people a year in her native village, claiming its victims from those over 30 years old.

The condition known as chronic bilharzia in modern medical terms is called "tego" locally. Traditionally, tego is attributed to adultery, explains Mwanauba. No one has died from it in the past year, she says.

"In the past, children were almost invariably plagued by worms and had to visit health clinics pretty frequently. Not any more. And the numbers of diarrhoea and vomiting cases have also fallen dramatically," she says. Health officials estimate there has been a 50% drop in the number of diarrhoea and vomiting cases since the KWAHO pump was installed.

> *'In the past, children were almost invariably plagued by worms and had to visit health clinics pretty frequently. Not any more.'*

Traditionally, children with these two complaints were believed by the villagers to be bewitched. But KWAHO community-based workers have gradually been persuading women to take their children to health clinics, says Mwanauba.

Standards of hygiene have also risen. Women have been encouraged to wash their water containers, dry their kitchen utensils on raised platforms out of reach of dirt and dust, cover their drinking water, and, where possible, build and make use of latrines and bathrooms.

Mwanauba is one of two community-based workers who have to visit 55 wells in Diani location where they train mothers to run and maintain the handpumps. Taking turns according to a pre-agreed roster, two women sweep around the village pump every day to ensure that the surroundings are clean. The villagers elect committees to manage all water-related affairs, under the supervision of the community-based workers.

The 'harambee' spirit

The educational programme consists of a series of workshops and seminars, organised jointly by community development officers and public health technicians under the ministries of health and water, says Mwanauba. This integrated approach is regarded as one of the main reasons for the project's success, and can be seen in other areas as well. At the village level, the "harambee" (pull together) spirit has improved.

"Among the questions I often get asked by communities which have enjoyed the benefits of a water project is: 'Now how do we go about getting a clinic?' I tell them that we in KWAHO do not have funds to help set up a clinic, but urge them to band together and work as a group to achieve their objective."

Mwanauba cites Galu and Muhaka primary schools which are being enlarged by such combined efforts, led mainly by women's groups whose members had themselves been brought together by the water project.

Before the KWAHO project, women in the Digo community stayed indoors as much as possible, according to tradition, to avoid contact with all men except their husbands, brothers and other male relatives. Now the women have broken with tradition and work closely with the men in the water project. The men and women are trained together, too, something which previously was also taboo.

And people from different villages who previously could not sit together in a spirit of co-operation to discuss issues of common interest now work jointly under the water project. They have become aware that together they stand to gain a great deal.

Villagers who participate in communal water ventures usually improve their economic status. The time they used to spend fetching water in the old way — KWAHO tries to site the water pumps less than a kilometre from where the people live — is spent weaving mats or roofing made from coconut palm leaves.

But still many problems

The income raised goes mainly towards school fees and to buy better food. And the free time available is used to grow vegetables in kitchen gardens.

Farming in the area is, however, restricted by poor soils and by the baboons and monkeys which ravage the crops.

Despite the improvements the villagers have enjoyed since 1984 and their greater freedom to become involved in gainful production, Kenya still faces many problems supplying water to its rural areas.

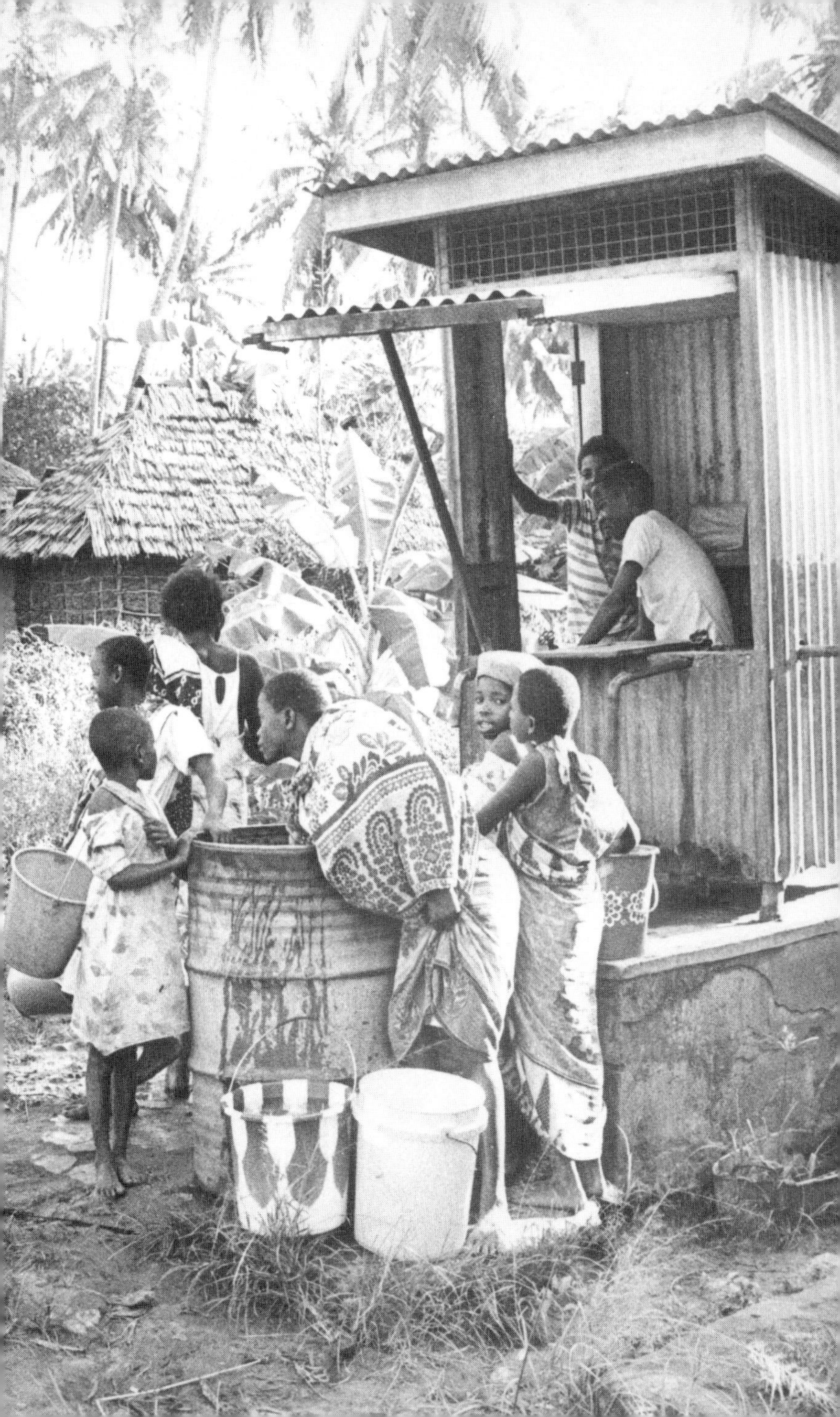

The plain fact is that the country's resources are inadequate and the finances available cannot meet the demand. And even in situations where funds for a project are available, delays occur due to inadequate manpower and the time it takes to expedite aspects of a scheme through the various official departments.

KWAHO tries to meet the problems by reaching communities where projects are to be implemented through teams of trained and experienced field workers. The teams combine sociologists and community-based workers (water-for-health assistants) whose approach to their work is a mixture of formal understanding and analysis with an informal, personal touch when dealing with the villagers.

The project in Kwale district has two sociologists and Rose Mulama is one of them. She serves as a programme officer and also as a training and liaison worker. But the project's nine extension workers are all locally-recruited non-professional people, of whom Mwanauba Omar is one.

One of the less successful handpumps; the wheel has to be turned laboriously by hand to bring up water.

Inappropriate technology is another problem area, with water pumps, engines and other machinery sometimes installed without due regard to whether spare parts are available or whether the villages concerned can afford them. This has a direct bearing on whether any particular water project proves to be sustainable in the long run. The sustainability is also affected by the type of pumps used.

The Kwale project tested 15 pumps over a two-year period to mid-1987, and the Afridev pump has proved to be the most efficient and popular make.

According to the project's senior programme officer, K. K. Munguti, the most costly aspect of water projects is the drilling of the borehole. This is done by the Water Ministry at a cost of between Ksh30,000 and 50,000 (US$1,875–3,125).

KWAHO provides the pumps, but the maintenance cost of Ksh187 per year (US$12) is left to the community to find.

Number of people per pump

Working on the assumption that each pump is designed to be used by some 250 people (40 families) and to last 10 years, each family pays only Ksh1 (6 US cents) per week to maintain it, says Munguti. The money collected above Ksh187 is put aside to meet emergencies, such as replacing a pump when it breaks down, which can cost between Ksh3,500 and 7,000 (US$220 - 440).

The Nira pump in Msambweni's Bomani village breaks down quite frequently because of the relatively large number of people living there. Pumps in villages with fewer people tend not to break down so often. Rose Maluma says people prefer the Nira pump because it is easy to operate and gives out plenty of water — only, however, where there is a high water table.

And that is the unspoken constraint on the sustainability of these water projects: the capacity of the subterranean acquifers to keep up their supplies. It is unwise to assume that they are infinite.

The Volonta pump has proved to be among the less successful hand pumps installed under the Kwale project. Dikirika village has a cement-covered well with the two parallel red wheels of the

Volonta mounted on it. The wheels have to be turned laboriously by hand to coax the water up, the contraption coughing out some of it each time the wheels turn completely.

It usually takes two girls working the wheels together to fill a bucket. You can see on their faces how tired they become as they turn the wheels round and round and watch the level of water slowly rising in the bucket under the spout of the pump.

The girls don't talk as they work the wheels with their arms. And for some reason the women in the long queue waiting their turn are also silent. They only start talking when the two girls have filled their bucket and carried it away.

Ongoing community involvement

Community participation per se is, however, not enough if KWAHO's experience is anything to go by. It must be coupled with ongoing community involvement for the entire lifespan of the project. KWAHO insists on exploiting local resources at the planning, implementation, maintenance and evaluation phases of the project.

Rose Maluma says that, in Kwale district, the villagers were involved from the word go. At the planning stage they were asked to identify their needs and priorities. They also participated, for example, in the siting of potential water points, taking into account cultural considerations, such as the mosques in Muslim communities where large numbers of worshippers perform the required ablutions before going in to pray.

One instance of this is the Volonta pump that was installed in Dikirika village about 6 metres (20 feet) in front of the Tawheed Islamic Centre. On their way to the mosque at prayer times, men roll up their sleeves and remove their fezzes as they approach the open water tank. They use a "tiw" (ladle made from half a coconut shell and a stick) to scoop up the water with which they wash their hands, faces and feet before entering the mosque.

According to Senior Programme Officer Munguti, KWAHO's success is attributable at least in part to the way it mobilises the local people. KWAHO, he says, is also integrated into the government system. Although the Water Ministry's head office is in Nairobi, it has administrative centres throughout the country.

"We KWAHO staff members use the same facilities — including offices and transport — at the disposal of the ministry officials. It is therefore hard to distinguish between the government officers and us, the NGOs. KWAHO staff are part and parcel of the decision-making process in the Kwale project. This way there is less conflict in the implementation of government policy."

Munguti, a sociologist, maintains that the main people who were supposed to benefit from the project — the women and children who jointly carry out the task of fetching water for their households — actually are benefiting.

In most communities, the water workers are two-thirds women. "Consequently the women, being in a position to take decisions that will benefit themselves and their children directly, do so," Munguti observes. He supports this statement by citing the employment trend at KWAHO's Kwale office. All the nine non-professional community-based workers are women.

How is success measured?

Munguti then launches into a discussion of the yardsticks used to measure the success of the Kwale project.

He starts by stressing the response of the community over a sustained period: three years. The initial excitement caused by the launch of a project dies away in many cases within a year, and with it the people's interest and commitment. But in Kwale, people still inquire about various aspects of the provision of water, he notes. And during the three years, the numbers of water committees that have been formed, and the numbers of self-help groups registered, have mushroomed.

KWAHO is no longer able to supervise all the work, due to shortage of staff, but the work is now being done quite competently by the locals, says Munguti.

In accordance with the district focus of its rural development policy, the government has readily agreed to finance the Kwale project now that the handpump pilot study has proved to be so successful. As a result, the pilot project, which covered only 50,000 people, is to be extended beyond Msambweni and Diani locations, to cover the whole of Kwale district whose population is estimated at 450,000.

Further evidence of the project's success, says Munguti, is KWAHO's plan to hand it over completely to the communities of the two locations. Currently, most of the villages in these two areas handle about 80% of their water affairs, including the security, maintenance and cleanliness of the pumps, as well as the finances and registration of their self-help groups.

> *'The pilot project is to be extended to cover the whole of Kwale whose population is estimated at 450,000.'*

The project has also had its failures, Munguti notes, giving the example of water committees which have not been consistent in these different aspects.

According to Project Manager L. Biwott, although KWAHO has succeeded in promoting the installation and use of handpumps in Kwale and elsewhere, it ought to open the communities' eyes to other realities: "KWAHO should try to motivate communities to move a step further and realise that the handpump is not a long-term solution to water problems."

People need to be informed about roof—rainwater catchment, dams, protection of springs and the augmentation of existing water supplies. Beyond the handpump, communities need to see the value of motorised pumps which, though more expensive, are easier to use and more efficient, requiring no exhausting physical labour.

Communities could also exploit Kenya's rural electrification programme to run diesel or electric pumps they manage to install, he says optimistically.

From modest beginnings, the KWAHO programme has initiated more than 100 water projects throughout Kenya. These projects have freed large numbers of Kenyan women from the daily toil of

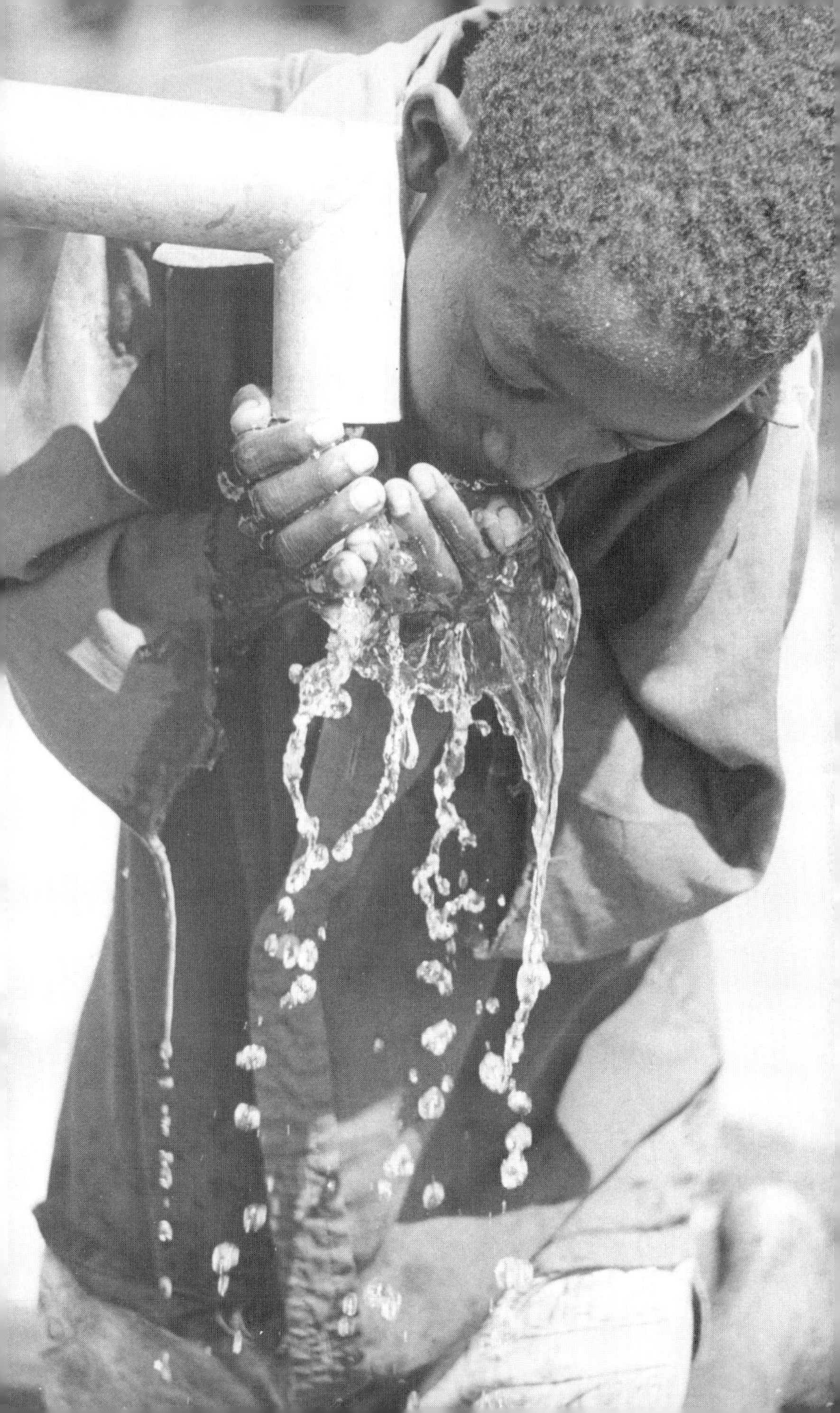

fetching and carrying water and have improved the quality of life of the villagers.

KWAHO's experiences challenge a major feeling within the development community: that NGOs should stick to small-scale, low cost projects. KWAHO has demonstrated that NGOs are more than capable of managing projects that have a wider reach as well.

SRI LANKA

GROWING TREES IN THE LIGHT OF THE BUDDHA

MALLIKA WANIGASUNDARA

SRI LANKA: Growing trees in the light of the Buddha

MALLIKA WANIGASUNDARA

More than 2,000 years ago the Buddha taught his followers to protect nature and live in harmony with it. "The forest," he said, "is a peculiar organisation of unlimited kindness and benevolence that makes no demands for its sustenance and extends generously the product of its life's activity. It offers protection to all beings, even to the axeman who destroys it."

But, although Sri Lankan society is deeply rooted in Buddhism, these teachings seem to have been forgotten. Cutting down forests, misusing water and abusing the soil have reached alarming proportions.

In 1956, forests covered almost 50% of Sri Lanka's land area. By 1983 it was only 27%. The poor help the rich to strip the forests of timber for a daily wage. Peasant farmers clear the forest to build homes and practise "chena" (slash and burn cultivation) to grow food crops and tobacco.

Deterioration of the environment is only one of many problems which engulf Sri Lanka. Others are poverty, population growth, landlessness, and bad housing. And all this has been made worse by the growing group violence of the past few years.

Rural poverty and joblessness dominate Sri Lanka's 23,000 villages where more than 75% of the people live. Half the total population of nearly 16 million depends on food stamps issued by the government for basic essentials. They have to, with average annual income at US$360 a head.

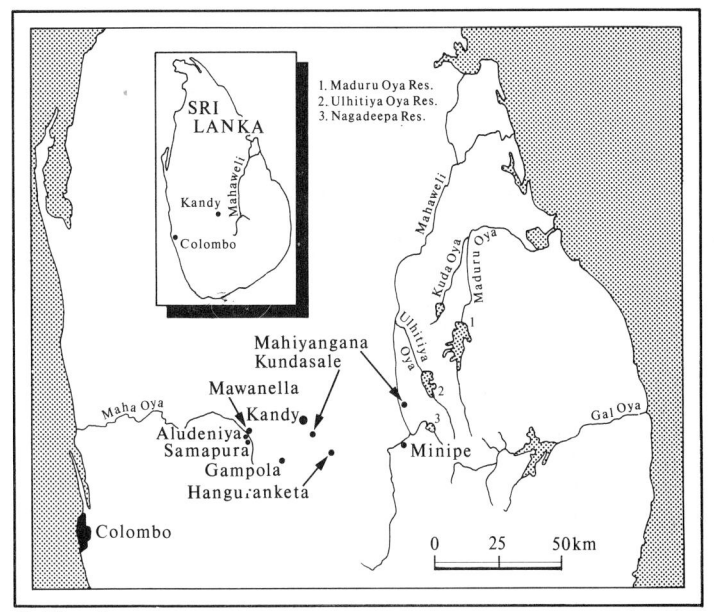

SRI LANKA: Growing trees in the light of the Buddha

Sri Lanka

This is the backdrop to the work of the Nation Builders Association of Sri Lanka (NBA), a non-governmental organisation with a profoundly Buddhist philosophy aimed at conservation and development.

NBA headquarters at Kundasale, nestled in the mountains of the central Kandy district, puts this philosophy in action. It is a haven of calm behind the concrete and semi-urban paraphernalia of the town.

The land, fashioned into ridges and reinforced embankments with paved paths and little ponds, boasts many rare indigenous trees and plants. In the sprawling nursery there are 80,000 seedlings for the reforestation programme.

Something to do in the vacation

NBA grew out of the predicament of a university student at the Peradeniya University at Kandy who was unable to return home for the vacation in the summer of 1963. He asked the Registrar, M.B. Adikaram, if he could stay on the campus.

The university rules did not permit this so the student stayed at a nearby Buddhist temple. But this started Adikaram thinking of all the students who could spend their vacations helping to improve their villages. "I started organising vacation work camps so that students could channel their restless energy into useful service," he says, "and this came to be known as the University Nation Builders Association."

The first work camps were short-term, modest projects based on the concept of aided self-help.

M.B. Adikaram, registrar of the Peradeniya University, Kandy, and founder of NBA.

"Ideals were high but funds were low," he explains. The students gave free labour to the villages — a system which has come to be known as "Shramadana".

More than 500 camps were held involving thousands of students. In 1967, for instance, about 2,000 students took part in groups of 25 to 50.

They went to work in desperately poor villages throughout the country. They rebuilt houses, toilets, wells and roads. They cleaned out irrigation canals, deepened channels, desilted tanks and helped with the harvesting of rice and drying of fish.

The villagers shared their rice and vegetables with the students. But the students were not popular at first: they were reputed to be unruly, undisciplined and irresponsible. Eventually they were accepted, and Adikaram felt he had achieved one of his aims — to improve the image of the students. "I was very pleased when a leading morning paper praised us in its editorial," he recalls.

NBA is born

By then, so many young people were interested that "University" was dropped from the name and the "Nation Builders Association" came into being. In those days, NBA was hampered by lack of funds and transport. Adikaram's Fiat was the only vehicle. He put his savings into the organisation and his house was the office. Now there is a fleet of vehicles.

The NBA also has official recognition: it was incorporated as an approved charity by Act of Parliament in 1982.

Its concern with Sri Lanka's environmental problems has led NBA to develop a special interest in conservation, reforestation, land use and water management. That goes together with its goal of helping poverty-stricken villagers to raise their living standards and improve their quality of life.

NBA headquarters are a haven of calm behind the concrete world of Kandy town, in central Sri Lanka.

The activities are intertwined. For until the villagers are given alternative ways to earn a living they will go on destroying forests and devastating hillsides to cultivate tobacco and other crops.

NBA's approach aims to give back to the village an economic order in which people take from nature what they need and conserve the rest for their children.

It is inspired by the Buddhist ethic. Indeed, when NBA begins working in a new area one of the first contacts it makes is with the chief "bikkhu" (priest) of the Buddhist temple — a crucial figure in village affairs.

The soil and water are protected and the forests are understood for their beneficial effect on people and the environment. At the same time, the importance of education and technological training is also recognised.

"We do not urge an unmixed return to the past which is clearly impossible and inadvisable," says Adikaram. "But we try to reinvest the village communities with some of the ethical, social and economic supports which made them dignified, self-reliant and happily organised entities. "In these villages, the artisans and craftsmen, artists and performers have lost a certain quality of life, which in the past made their work not merely a means of livelihood but also the fulfilment of an innermost urge for creation.

"Each person was an artist lovingly pursuing a piece of work which was not a dreary chore, but was something akin to what the modern person pursues during leisure. There was no dichotomy between work and leisure as we know it now."

Blacksmiths and potters

In 1970 the programme changed from short-term work camps to long-term projects with financial assistance from outside. The first of these was the MOKO project which was backed by the Freedom from Hunger Campaign.

This involved 110 villages comprising mainly potters and blacksmiths situated between the Maha Oya (river) and Kuda Oya — hence MOKO — in a 78 square kilometre (30 square mile) area near the towns of Mawanella and Gampola.

Both the potters and the blacksmiths were getting poorer because of competition and inadequate technologies. NBA set out to improve their technical skills and working conditions. Volunteers from Thailand and Bangladesh, and students from the universities of Cambridge in Britain, and Maryland and Boston in the United States, lent a hand.

The 39 blacksmith families were given 13 workshops with modern equipment as part of a light engineering project. The villages were provided with electricity and for the first time the blacksmiths were able to use power hammers. A revolving fund of Rupees 40,000 (US$1,380) was set up so that they could draw small loans.

The blacksmiths have gone from strength to strength. One village, Samanpura, has become a small township with well-built houses instead of tumbledown cottages with dirty work areas.

NBA workshops and loans have revived the blacksmith tradition in several villages and prosperity has followed.

Everywhere the smiths are busy using their power tools to make agricultural implements and other hardware. Their products include pickaxes, crowbars, axes, knives, nuts and bolts, railings, grilles, brackets and wheelbarrows. The quality is high. They get orders from the Electricity Board for nuts, bolts and brackets, and they supply wheelbarrows to the Building Materials Corporation.

One of their leaders, Abaran Appu, although now old and sick, has the satisfaction of seeing his village and family prospering. Three of his sons are also blacksmiths, one with a workshop in the town and another with a shop in the capital, Colombo.

But that success cannot be guaranteed is shown by the potters. The five villages where the potters lived when NBA first made contact with them were in a sorry state, with dilapidated dwellings, no modern turn wheels, no land from which they could get a regular supply of clay and no marketing facilities.

The NBA helped them to rebuild their houses and each family was given a workshop. New turn wheels were introduced, although there was some resistance to these. Land was obtained from which they could get clay and they were given training to improve their products.

But, these many years later, there is only limited improvement. The younger generation, especially those who have been educated, have little enthusiasm for the craft.

Their ailing leader, P.G. Naide of Aludeniya, now has no obvious source of income and lives with his wife and unmarried daughter in the workshop provided by NBA. The rest of the house is falling down and there is no work under way.

There are no signs of a flourishing pottery industry in the villages — no mounds of clay or drying pots. Some families have sold or rented their workshops to others and most of them work mainly in the fields, especially at harvest-time.

Jobs for young people

But on the successful side again, NBA's reforestation programmes provide young people with jobs as well as training. They can earn just over Rs1,000 (US$34) a month.

SRI LANKA: Growing trees in the light of the Buddha

Former unemployed women participate in programmes to reforest the denuded regions of central Sri Lanka.

At its Kundasale headquarters, the leaders train in silviculture — the cultivation of trees — and are then put in charge of blocks of land of around 101 hectares (250 acres) where they plant trees, using the casual labour of young people from surrounding villages.

Women play a significant role in NBA affairs and are particularly known for their skill in creating tree-nurseries. One of them, Kamala Sriyalatha Jayasiri, began as a volunteer in the reforestation programme of the Victoria Project — part of the Accelerated Mahaweli Scheme, the diversion of the country's longest river for irrigation, power generation and increased food production.

She then studied forestry, soil conservation and nursery-keeping — from seed collection and soil preparation to manuring and the control of pests — as well as management and office skills. Now she is the project manager at Kundasale.

At the Buddhankotte nursery in the Mahiyangana area — one of three run by NBA — W.C. Heenmenike is among the key workers. Like Kamala, she says that it was NBA voluntary activities in which she took part after leaving school which made her realise the importance of saving the forests.

Tree-shaded oasis

The result of her contribution can be seen: the approach to Buddhankotte is through parched, dry land with wilting trees and outcrops of rock. In contrast, the nursery, run by 12 men and women, is a tree-shaded oasis with a man-made lake covered in water lilies. Planting begins in the rainy season and in preparation for it the nursery propagates 80,000 seedlings.

Heenmenike's father is a farmer and she is one of eight children. She has managed to save Rs10,000 (US$344) from her monthly salary of Rs1,000 (US$34) and has used this to add two rooms to the family's house.

Another member of the nursery staff, Iranganie Wickramaarachi, has used her salary to support a family of seven since her father died. She also manages to save.

Sri Lanka's forests are depleting at a rapid rate: more than 42,000 hectares (104,000 acres) a year have been destroyed since the

SRI LANKA: Growing trees in the light of the Buddha

NBA raises some funds by selling local plant species to the government and NGOs.

mid-1950s. Apart from clearing forests for timber and crops, large areas are obliterated as part of major development projects, such as the Mahaweli Scheme.

Millions of tons of topsoil have been washed away from these lands over the years due to deforestation. The removal of the forests from the upper reaches of the Mahaweli not only threatens the productivity of the scheme, but could lead to increased sedimentation through soil erosion, silting up the river and reservoirs and clogging the sluices.

Since 1982, NBA has been carrying out reforestation programmes in the upper catchment areas of the river. By 1984 the association had forested 1,828 hectares (4,517 acres). During the next year, no less than 1,587 hectares (3,920 acres) were planted.

Together with the Mahaweli Development Authority and with funds from the United States Agency for International Development (USAID), NBA is now reforesting the banks of the 39-kilometre, concrete-lined Minipe canal which takes water from the Mahaweli to the Ulhitiya and Maduru Oya reservoirs. Construction of the canal — with excavation, tree-felling and soil erosion — has left ugly scars on the landscape.

Some areas have also been devastated by fires caused by drought or carelessness. Jayatilleke Perera, project manager of the NBA programme, also blames fishermen who light fires at night while they are fishing: NBA's fire prevention squads do not operate at night. Still more damage is caused by the farmers who slash and burn the forests to grow crops.

The recovery project covers an area of nearly 1,300 hectares (3,210 acres) and since 1984 NBA has reforested more than 1,100 hectares (2,700 acres). NBA leaders organise and supervise the planting, using young people from the villages. They tend the plants for three years, replacing any that die.

Tree survival rates are now 60-80% — an improvement on the 50-60% of earlier years. But damage by cattle is still heavy, says Perera, especially since the drought. For when the usual grazing areas dry up the villagers allow their cattle to roam freely.

NBA workers admit that there is some resentment among villagers who regard the plantation areas as their grazing lands. They do not understand the need to stabilise the banks of the canal. "We are trying to combat

> *'The children have proved useful in acting as intermediaries.'*

these attitudes by talking to the villagers, and particularly schoolchildren," says Perera. The children have proved useful in acting as intermediaries. Some people are now coming forward to help protect the plantations.

But ultimately the villagers will have to be given alternative grazing lands if the plantations are to be properly protected, according to Lalitha Colombage, one of the Minipe leaders with experience in reforesting.

Tree ... to water

From tree-planting NBA's activities also naturally stretch to water. Although Sri Lanka is dotted with reservoirs and rivers, water management poses some problems. Water is still a scarce resource which needs to be shared fairly. Most farmers over-use water but the problem is especially acute among settlers in areas opened up by new irrigation schemes.

Good water management depends on good inter-community relations, training and the efforts of both farmers and irrigation officials, argues J.M.A. Jaywardene, who manages NBA's Nagadeepa "wewa" (reservoir) water management pilot project in Mahiyangana.

Unless farmers are fully involved in the operation and maintenance of the irrigation network, he says, settlement schemes can face serious problems with tragic waste of water. The problems faced by the Nagadeepa irrigation scheme before NBA set up its pilot project show what can go wrong without proper management.

The Nagadeepa reservoir, 19 kilometres (11.8 miles) from Mahiyangana, was completed in 1968. It could hold 27,000 acre-feet of water and about 2,000 farmers depended on it to cultivate more than 1,600 hectares (4,000 acres) of land.

The farmers were poor and settled there expecting to reap two harvests a year with the help of the new irrigation network. But 17 years later, many of them were no better off. Those with plots near the reservoir were taking all the water, leaving none for the farmers further down the line. Even when there was enough water in the reservoir for two seasons, some farmers could not manage one harvest.

Angry and frustrated, some farmers abandoned their plots. Channels became clogged, banks crumbled and water was diverted privately by those with the power to do it. The "jala palakas" (water supervisors) favoured some and ignored others.

The irrigation officials did what they could but were unable to prevent the fights which developed. The regular "kanna" meetings where schedules were discussed for water releases, ploughing and planting invariably turned into slanging matches.

When the water was released the farmers took up crude weapons and tried to take what they could by force. Planting timetables laid down at the meetings were never followed and the sluice gates were opened at the whim of certain individuals.

Faced by this chaos, the Irrigation Department and NBA launched a pilot water management project at Nagadeepa in 1985 with funds from USAID and the government. Farmers' committees were set up to manage and maintain the irrigation network. The farmers do most of the work themselves through the "shramadana" (self-help) system, including rebuilding banks, maintaining channels and repairing sluices. The maintenance work is done by the Irrigation Department and by private contractors.

> *'Now we decide what seed material we need, how much water, and when and what repairs should be done.'*

The farmers now feel responsible for the irrigation system and realise that, if they work together, everyone benefits. The antagonism between farmers and irrigation officials has given way to greater understanding and co-operation.

As well as the farmers' committees there are 12 community organisations whose representatives have been trained by NBA to act as links between farmers and officials.

The NBA worked hard to create the new community spirit, organising "Ran karal" (harvest) and "Aluth sahal" (sharing) ceremonies as well as several "shramadana" campaigns to encourage a sense of ownership with regard to the irrigation networks.

Even the "kanna" meetings have become constructive with the farmers bringing proposals and taking decisions instead of officials handing out orders. "Now we decide what seed material we need, how much water, and when and what repairs should be done," one farmer explains.

New leadership qualities are emerging. The farmers realise that NBA will not be there forever and that, eventually, they will have to take over the complete management of the system themselves.

Material benefits

According to an evaluation made by USAID and NBA in mid-1987, most Nagadeepa farmers are now cultivating two crops each year. By March 1987, 540 farmers had benefited directly from the project, 2,700 people had received indirect benefits and 91 farmers had been trained.

Yields have increased from 2.06 - 3.6 tonnes per hectare to 3.6 - 6.2 tonnes. Project manager Jayawardene estimates that in "maha" (the main season) they make about Rs14,000 (US$483). In "yala" (the second season) they make about Rs10,000 (US$344) by growing subsidiary crops like green gram, soya, chillies, cowpeas, onions and other vegetables.

The increased incomes are obvious as new houses replace the old huts, or families stock up with bricks and tiles. D.M. Gunasekera is typical. Previously, he could never cultivate during both seasons and even now he can only manage one of the two acres he owns. But the 3.9 tonnes per hectare he gets from that plot has enabled him to rebuild his house.

The farmers also feel confident enough to take advantage of the small Rs7,500 (US$258) loans which the Housing Development Authority offers families in rural areas.

Grazing ground shortage

One of the problems which still needs a solution in Nagadeepa is the lack of grazing grounds for the animals. There are three grazing grounds at present but these are not enough, especially in times of drought.

Marketing is also difficult. The farmers are obliged to sell to middlemen at low prices because there is no efficient marketing system. The NBA is hoping to help them devise a new system in the future.

Because the Nagadeepa reservoir is rainfed and has no rivers running into it, water is sometimes scarce, even when it is properly shared.

For some time the farmers have been urging that the reservoir be augmented with water from Gal Oya; the government has now agreed to use foreign funding to do it. The farmers would never have achieved this before NBA showed them how to work together.

With the experience gained at Nagadeepa, NBA is launching other water management projects at Minipe and Pimburettewa. And farmers are already being trained for another project at Hanguranketa.

The NBA is the only NGO which has a water management institute. Based at the Kundasale centre, it trains both farmers and officials and works closely with the Irrigation Department.

The subjects covered in the seven-day courses are the irrigation distribution system, crop development and the scheduling of water; estimating water use; and the role of farmers. The courses also look at Sri Lanka's water resources and the foundations of its agriculture; technology transfer; the improvement of cultivation practices; leadership; and relations between farmers and irrigation officials.

The value of the courses is shown in the experience of 20 young farmers from Hanguranketa, all of them the sons of farmers, who have worked in the fields with their fathers. They admit they were involved in disputes over water and feel responsible for some of the fights which broke out in the past. But they say the course has made them realise the importance of operating the irrigation system collectively.

"We cannot expect the Irrigation Department to do everything for us," says a young farmer. "We have to look after the system ourselves and we have to take this message back to the village."

One of NBA's problems is its need for more trained managers and administrators, including supervisors "All our projects suffer because of this," explains the founder, M.B. Adikaram.

NBA trains people, but they invariably leave as the projects they are working on draw to a close. In any case, the organisation cannot afford to keep a large full-time staff on its payroll. But NBA is now looking at ways of giving

'We cannot expect the Irrigation Department to do everything for us. We have to look after the system ourselves and we have to take this message back to the village.'

its personnel security of tenure and other benefits, like provident fund contributions, to encourage them to stay.

NBA also suffers from a lack of staff proficient in English — a real handicap for an organisation which is heavily dependent on funding from abroad.

NBA has received funds from both governmental and non-governmental sources. It now undertakes work worth around Rs10 million (US$344,330) a year. Much of this is paid as wages to the young people working on forestry and other projects. Adikaram estimates that about 100,000 people have taken part in NBA projects or have benefited from them financially.

The future

The Sri Lankan Government is about to embark on a major development programme in the watershed of the Mahaweli River. The project includes all aspects of conservation and land use. Training will be offered in forestry; nursery management; soil conservation; the cultivation of grass and fodder crops, spices, flowers and palms; setting up agro-based industries, poultry-farming, dairy farming and bee-keeping.

Five pilot projects will be set up in the hill country and other climatic zones. NBA will be working on these. Training programmes have started, involving government farms and centres as well as NBA's facilities. The Buddha taught that the destruction of even a plant was an act of misconduct and this was underpinned by the broader philosophy of "ahisma", or non-violence. The Buddha and his disciples found serenity for meditation in woods, parks and forests. NBA seeks to create an environment where peace and prosperity can again prevail.

Under the conditions prevailing in Sri Lanka, NBA, as a non-sectarian, non-political organisation, faces an awesome task in remaining true to its ideals. So far it seems to have succeeded.

ZAMBIA

THE SAME HANDS,
BUT NEW MINDS

JOHN MUKELA

ZAMBIA:
The same hands, but new minds

JOHN MUKELA

Thomas Chishimba leans back in his chair and smiles. "When I first came to this area, they were suspicious that I would complicate their work," he says. "But I think they have realised my role is merely complementary."

He was talking about provincial members and leaders of Zambia's ruling United National Independence Party (UNIP) and their initial reaction to an organisation which was, when set up in 1980, known as the Mungwi Village Industry Service (MVIS).

MVIS has since been re-christened and the new name — Village Development Foundation (VDF) — may conjure up for some the image of a huge urban-based bureaucracy with little in common with any rural village.

But, in fact, VDF is continuing to fulfil its original purpose: to reappraise and try to solve the problems of poverty in Zambia — which, of course, also plague many other countries in Africa too.

VDF has been making its contribution to the nation's wellbeing by focusing on an aspect of Zambian reality which does not often receive attention from the central authorities: it has devoted all its energies to the daily struggle for existence of people in remote villages and homesteads in the country's Northern Province, where there is hardly any modern infrastructure and it sometimes seems the inhabitants have been forgotten.

Chishimba drives home the point in vivid terms: "In rural areas,"

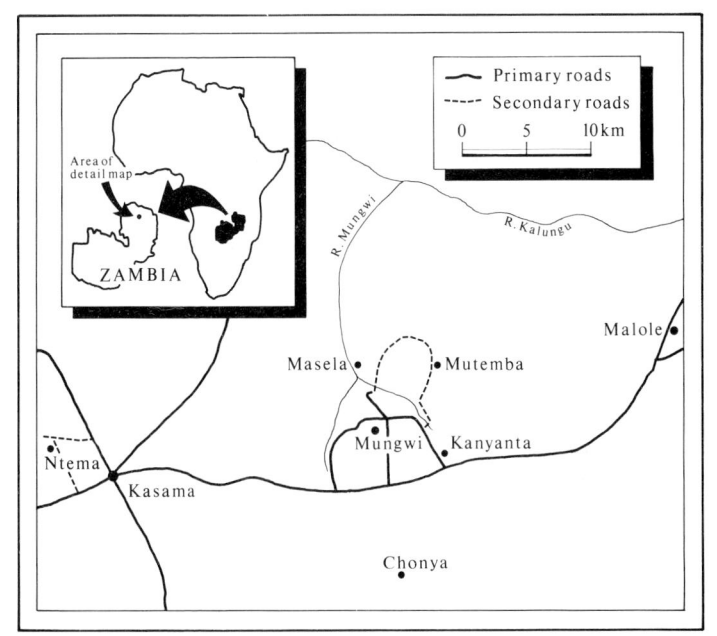

Northern Zambia

he says, "most of the people have no idea that they are living in an independent country. They have no conception whatsoever that they are part of a nation which has relations with neighbouring countries and with countries beyond the sea. Their political awareness is just about non-existent. As for their economic status and standard of life, that's even worse."

New farming methods

Zambia's Northern Province is not an area as prone to drought as other parts of the continent. It has fairly good soils and annual rainfall which the records show to be among the highest in the country. Nevertheless, the province's agricultural production has historically left much to be desired.

The farmers have until recently relied on techniques such as the use of hoes to till the land. That approach is now slowly changing. When their rare cash savings allow, they buy small amounts of fertiliser to help cultivate indigenous crops such as cassava or millet.

And the emergent modern small-scale farmer who hires a tractor for ploughing to augment the efforts of oxen is having results which have begun to influence the attitudes of the old-fashioned cultivators and to draw their attention to the productivity of hybrid seeds.

But a major constraint on crop yields in Northern Province, as in other parts of Africa and the South, is the practice known locally as "chitemene" — slashing and burning trees to clear the land for farming.

Chitemene involves clearing a small area of forest, burning some of the felled vegetation and leaving the rest to decompose and gradually release nutrients into the soil. By growing a mixture of crops, farmers can make maximum use of nutrients. Nevertheless, productivity of most soils declines markedly within two or three years and the farmer moves to clear a new area.

As long as population remains low and land can lie fallow for at least 10 years, shifting cultivation is a sustainable system. Problems arise when the population increases. Then farmers exhaust the land to the point at which the soil is permanently degraded and becomes useless for forestry or agriculture.

The government has not been notably successful in providing alternatives to chitemene. And its various programmes to upgrade agriculture have failed because they were not pitched at the village level and did not have the villagers as the primary beneficiaries.

A growing proportion of government spending on agriculture has gone, not into the production of food itself, but to subsidise the low price of food for Zambia's townspeople, and the purchase of agricultural goods, including fertilisers, for large state farms.

Limited impact

The impact of government spending has, in any event, been small for reasons which include the absence of a stable and efficient organisational framework, the lack of a skilled workforce in the agricultural sector, as well as inadequate transport and marketing facilities.

That the rapid developments in the urban sector have induced a high proportion of younger and better-educated Zambians to migrate to the towns has not benefited the countryside either.

A further negative factor of particular importance to small-scale farmers has, until very recently, been the low prices paid to the producers. It simply wasn't worthwhile being a farmer; the prices received were barely enough to cover the cost of producing the crops. Nor was there a system which ensured that the farmers were promptly and reliably paid.

'It simply wasn't worthwhile being a farmer; the prices received were barely enough to cover the cost of producing the crops.'

Agricultural prices, in terms of the amount of manufactured goods which they would buy — the rural/urban terms of trade — actually declined by an average of about two-thirds between 1965 and 1980. The fall in prices for the foodstuffs which the poorer farmers tend to produce — cassava, sorghum, finger and bush millet, and honey — was even greater.

So that was the background — lack of knowledge about problems confronting rural people, poverty, and grandiose dreams in urban offices — against which the VDF came into being in 1980.

An individual vision

Establishment of the VDF owes much to the vision and efforts of 42-year-old Thomas Chishimba who resigned as Senior Administrative Officer in Zambia's Ministry of Labour and Social Services "principally because of what I had seen and experienced overseas".

Chishimba says a 12-month stay in Israel was of immense benefit to his understanding: "I saw and learnt how the Israelis solve unemployment at village level. That is of particular interest because I see the village, if unassisted, as a source of major trouble for the urban areas."

He was, he says, also inspired by what he saw during his stay in Canada's Northwest Territories: "At one village in Fort Resolution, where I lived for six months, a group of people started a club whose main feature was the sawmill they owned. The government later helped them to acquire a bigger machine.

"They make and sell cut-wood planks of all sizes, and draw their wages from the income the unit earns. From what I saw, the 75 people in the village all work at the sawmill. The youth don't even bother going to Edmonton or Toronto to look for jobs. And when they go away to visit friends and relations, they always come back to carry on the work."

Thomas Chishimba, — he overcame suspicions in founding the VDF.

"That experience," Chishimba explains, "made me feel I should try it in my country. That was when I thought of leaving government service."

VDF's objectives

VDF's headquarters, and Chishimba's office, are in a rented single room on the first floor of a building in Kasama, the provincial capital. It is from there, in very cramped conditions, that the VDF programme is articulated, planned and implemented.

Generally speaking, VDF seeks to transform the social life of Zambia's rural areas, and it hopes to do so by achieving its programme objectives, which are to:

- Promote income-generating small-scale cottage industries in rural villages and so create employment.
- Dissuade the youth from migrating to urban areas.

- Bring basic services to the rural areas which will facilitate the necessary economic development.
- Encourage a spirit of self-reliance as the psychological springboard to development.
- Provide adult education sufficient to create awareness among the participating villagers of some of the causes of their plight and suffering, and to instil the will to overcome the difficulties in co-operation with their neighbours.
- Train the locals in more efficient food production techniques and organise them to start producer co-operatives in rural areas.

VDF currently has a staff of 18, from field officers and voluntary teachers to a carpentry instructor and a mechanic. All the organisation's volunteers receive a monthly living allowance of K160 (US$20).

The project area

So far, VDF has set up resource centres in seven villages in the remote Malole area of Northern Province, north of the Muchinga Mountains and due east of Kasama.

The area, which usually enjoys high rainfall from November to March, is heavily wooded, mainly with miombo trees (*Pterocarpus Angolensis*), but also some evergreen forests. The woodlands provide woodfuel and are bountiful sources of caterpillars, a traditional delicacy. Although the soils tend to have their nutrients carried away by the rains — they become leached — it is not significant within any single growing season.

The area also enjoys abundant water for irrigation, from streams and swamps. Most of the streams can be diverted for furrow irrigation with minimum investment. And the swamps are suitable for growing rice. Piped water is, however, very limited; villagers obtain their supplies from streams and wells.

The total population of the seven project villages is estimated at about 12,500, about 54% of whom are female.

VDF's resource centres are located deep in bush territory, away from the nearest urban area.

At the Home Industries project in Ntema village, a few kilometres out of Kasama, a new building is used for meetings and activities which were previously held under the inadequate shelter of trees. The project began in May 1983 and is aimed at improving the quality of life, mainly of women and children, through a pre-school and a dressmaking and tailoring unit.

VDF first concentrated on a group of men and women at Ntema who had earlier been members of a literacy class. The reason for this narrow focus was to ensure that only committed people were involved.

There is now a project committee of four which includes the village headman, Ntema. The teacher, Mrs Gertrude Musenga, provides her services on a voluntary basis.

The village community was itself largely instrumental in identifying the need for, and initiating, both the pre-school and sewing projects. Of the two, they believe the pre-school to be of greater benefit. It provides no marketable skills to members but is considered important to the future welfare of the children and their families as a whole. More than 70 children have been enrolled.

The centre is also the venue of the area's four-week training course for pre-school teachers organised jointly by VDF and Kasama District Council.

Improving literacy

The effectiveness of this course is indicated by the fact that children with no history of any schooling in their families are able to write their names and count up to 20 within three months.

An adult literacy class is held in the same venue, and a number of adults can now read and write. Their excitement and the pride in their achievement is moving to witness.

As part of its functional literacy approach, VDF teaches people to read in conjunction with their farming chores, the texts being about work, use of inputs, and so on. The benefit of this method is that the dignity of the adults is left intact; they are not made to feel on a par with their children.

One can gauge the community's commitment from the contributions of time, energy and money to the construction of the resource centre's building. Supplying their labour free of charge, they mixed scarce cement with sand and made the bricks. They also pay 50ngwee (about 6UScents) per child per month to augment the VDF grant.

The centre is used as a meeting-place where discussions are held concerning village welfare.

As for the dressmaking and tailoring sessions held on the same premises, VDF supplies the cloth, cotton and needles. For a short period, it also provided a volunteer instructor. The participating women are generally enthusiastic, but view the use of needles as "slow". They are keen to

'Their excitement and the pride in their achievement is moving to witness.'

acquire sewing machines, and funds are being raised for this and to buy weaving looms.

Meanwhile, their pride in the project is obvious. "We can now mend our children's clothes, so they don't have to go about wearing torn garments," they say. "We can cut interesting designs for dresses by following patterns. And when the men ask, we sometimes make alterations to their trousers."

One of the project's beneficiaries is Mrs Mary Chanda: "Thanks to the centre, I can now read and write. As for food, I grow maize and beans. My family produces about 16 bags of maize [One bag of maize weighs 50 kilos/112 pounds.] per acre (0.4 hectare) ."

Working together

Another VDF project — one of the most successful — is about 90 kilometres (55 miles) from Kasama at a place called Matale Wa Kabwe in the Chonya district.

Here, the community services are more integrated with crop production. This is largely because a parallel scheme was being run by the Catholic Archdiocese of Kasama when VDF began work in the area in 1981. The scheme is called "Cinci wa Babili" in the local

Bemba language and means "working together".

In close collaboration with VDF, the Cinci scheme has significantly changed the economic face of the Chonya area by introducing a balanced combination of activities aimed at developing agriculture and establishing co-operatives.

> *'The farmers are so well-off that they now pay market prices for their transport and run their own credit union to meet their finance requirements.'*

The work has involved organising farmers to be shown new agricultural practices in the field, encouraging the adoption of such practices, and training particular individuals to set up co-operatives so that they may eventually assume leadership roles. The project also arranges the supply of inputs from outside and the marketing of surplus grain.

Cinci is headed by Brother John Beaudry, whose development work in the Kasama area spans many years.

According to Brother John, the development of co-operatives outside the Cinci project is in a state of stagnation.

"In the past, co-operatives were organised under the Northern Co-operative Union which was sponsored by the government," he says. But because those co-ops were set up, not to promote better farming methods or to improve the members' well-being, but as a means of extracting their produce, the villagers' interest soon evaporated.

"Without clear benefits coming back to the local farmers, those co-operatives quickly became dormant."

The Cinci project, in contrast, is remarkable for the way in which it has transformed Chonya into a self-sustaining collection of villages where the farmers are so well-off that they now pay market prices for their transport and run their own credit union to meet their finance requirements.

At Matale Wa Kabwe, 42-year-old Samuel Mulenga described

ZAMBIA: *The same hands, but new minds*

'We had no cultivation like this — just maize and finger millet. Now, we plant cabbages, onions, tomatoes and other vegetables.'

to me what things were like before: "We had no cultivation like this — just maize and finger millet. Now, as you can see, we plant cabbages, onions, tomatoes and other vegetables, as well as maize."

Mulenga believes the ingredients for the area's development were present for a long time, just waiting to be tapped. What was needed for the villagers to start exploiting the available resources for their own benefit was a different attitude of mind, a stronger belief in their own ability to do things for themselves.

He points to one of the furrows he and his neighbours have dug from the river as channels for irrigation: "We could have dug these furrows long ago. We always had enough labour to do the job. These are the same hands we had then," he smiles, raising his palms. "But our minds hadn't been prepared."

A clinic at Kanyanta

Another village-oriented development programme initiated by VDF is in an area called Kanyanta. The villagers have erected an impressive community hall, a shop, and a building which houses the mill for grinding maize.

The hall is also used as an ante-natal clinic, and provides space for a pre-school and for adult literacy purposes. As well as being the venue where community matters are discussed, it is the place where a whole range of cottage industries are encouraged — dressmaking, jam-making, soap-making, cookery and other income-generating skills. Women are also taught the basics of childcare and personal hygiene.

The project has created employment for 22 women, most of whom have completed primary school. They are paid K2 (25US cents) per eight-hour shift and earn on average K60 (US$7.50) a month. The Kanyanta carpentry and joinery project caters mainly for handicapped children who have dropped out of primary school.

They are taught and encouraged to make chairs, beds, brooms, doors, door and window frames and tables. Fifteen boys have so far been employed, also at a rate of K2 per eight-hour shift.

The adult literacy programme seeks to make its 28 members "functionally literate" and most of them can now read and write.

As for the children, 23 of them were accepted into grade one of primary school after attending the pre-school which had prepared them for regular schooling. In 1985 there were 24 grade one entries and there are at present 48 children in the pre-school.

On the agricultural side, the Kanyanta community is encouraged to grow soyabeans and in 1987 they were induced with incentives to cultivate castor oil seeds as raw materials for the manufacture of soap and body oils.

Changing attitudes

VDF finds that people are gradually changing their attitudes. B. Bwalya, chairman of the Cinci wa Babili scheme in Chonya, embodies the new outlook. At 55, Bwalya is seen by locals as a symbol of success.

Although not in favour of traditional chitemene, he maintains that those farmers who still farm that way do so "only because that's the way of life here and they have no money for fertiliser".

For one who barely three years before had almost nothing to show for his labours, Bwalya was in 1987 able to harvest 213 bags of maize, raising K16,000 (US$2,000) from the proceeds. After repaying debts, he had K5,000 (US$625) in hand. He has built a comfortable brick family house and wishes to buy a utility van to transport produce to Kasama, 80 kilometres (50 miles) away.

'The shortage of labour limits development.'

It is certainly possible to say that VDF is well on its way to achieving its aims. It is nevertheless true that there is still a long way to go.

One of the difficulties the area faces is the shortage of labour which places a definite limit on the amount of development that can take place. A high proportion of the households consist of elderly villagers, with many of the able-bodied youths heading for the urban Copperbelt in search of jobs as soon as they can. The youngsters who remain are still at school and only work on the farms part-time.

This problem should not be over-stated, however. There is clear evidence that more fifth-form school-leavers are deciding to stay in the countryside and work on the land as farmers.

An example is 24-year-old Willbrod Mulenga, who helps his grandfather Samuel. Together they have dug a furrow to irrigate their field and are cultivating an impressive patch of vegetables and maize. Willbrod, still unmarried, completed form five at school and this is his first season as a farmer.

Thomas Chishimba believes, meanwhile, that he and his colleagues should place greater emphasis on adult education. In a VDF report, he notes that the amount of development in rural areas is very much less than that found in urban areas "because adult education was never given to the rural population".

Colonial use of force

Articulating this problem, Chishimba points to the use of force by the colonial authorities in implementing various rural programmes, without bothering to give adequate explanations.

The Masela bakery has provided the community with a regular source of income.

As an example, he cites fear as the prime reason behind the failure of pit latrine programmes during colonial times. Rural communities, he says, built latrines only because they were afraid of being fined or imprisoned by the district commissioners. But the people did not actually use the latrines because they felt these had been foisted on them.

Chishimba adds that inadequate adult education and fear "have combined to kill people's initiative in rural villages, and illiteracy keeps compounding the damage. Consequently, it's not easy to change people's minds. It's an uphill struggle requiring sound training methods to remove the fear and facilitate the entry of new ideas into their awareness. But until people do understand the need for change, there is little chance of developing the rural areas."

VDF therefore places high on its list of priorities the creation of awareness through adult education.

"People should learn and understand the reasons behind their project," Chisimba says. "Motivating people first before erecting buildings, for example, is of paramount importance in bringing about the required commitment and development. Buildings such as community halls and small-scale factories will function efficiently only when the people who are supposed to run them feel confident in what they are doing."

The Masela bakery success

The effectiveness of this approach is easily gauged from the successful way in which the bakery project was implemented in Masela village.

It began in 1983 when VDF made people aware that bread-making could help control and then reverse the high rate of malnutrition among children, and at the same time provide the community with an ongoing source of income. Instead of carrying bulky "nshima" (cooked maize meal) to school, children could take bread.

Preliminary discussions were held, and it was only after the fourth community meeting that the villagers agreed to initiate the scheme.

AGAINST ALL ODDS

VDF projects have also created jobs for at least 400 women in the villages.

A committee was elected to manage the project, mediate between participants and resolve any misunderstandings. Skilled manpower came from the village itself in the form of six ex-cooks who had migrated back from the Copperbelt where they had worked both in government and private institutions.

The first practical step was to construct a pole and grass-roofed shelter. This was done, but the project participants later decided to build a permanent building to house the bakery. Ten men and 26 women were involved in this work. They made bricks, and also pans for baking the bread from empty cooking-oil tins. A management was set up and a bank account opened.

At each step, project participants meet to discuss and plan their work programme. They intend to register the bakery as a primary producer co-operative, and are investigating the pros and cons of introducing jam-making as an extension of the project.

Says Chishimba: "It's a small project but it meets the needs of the people and motivates them to grow wheat for which there is now a local market."

Chishimba firmly believes VDF's work has been successful so far because it has not only mobilised villagers to do things for themselves, but it has done so in a way that renders the projects sustainable.

"From our seven years' experience," he says, "the first schemes are still operating and still have their membership. People are working on their own and for the past four years we have provided 300 places for children to enter primary school after pre-school. In home industry, we have created jobs for 400 women. And people can now get as many bags of maize as they need."

The farmers have their own views

Many of the farmers agree that they are in principle capable of standing on their own feet, of carrying on the schemes VDF has helped them to get started.

They also do have other views. Lazarus Chikwe of Chikwe village feels, for example, that the main problem is the difficulty in getting enough fertiliser. Noah Kalulu, at Chimba village, concurs.

Because most of the project villages are located in such remote terrain, and because VDF does not have money to splash around, deliveries of fertiliser to the farmers who are keen to break out of the chitemene system are at best erratic.

And the farmers have to travel all the way to Kasama to get their produce to market. But the entrepreneur at Cinci wa Babili has figured out a way to solve this problem — a locally owned pick-up van.

> *'Many of the farmers agree that they are in principle capable of standing on their own feet, of carrying on the schemes VDF has helped them to get started.'*

Another problem that bulks very large in the lives of the locals is the inadequate water supply. At Chimba Primary School, which caters for 350 pupils, shortage of water is a perpetual hardship.

The community it serves has access to only one well whose concrete surrounding is cleaned twice a week, on Mondays and

Wednesdays. "But when the children are at home during the holidays, the cleaning stops," says one teacher. "The well is about a kilometre from here. About 50 households use it."

Some of the teachers at the school feel that organisations such as VDF tend to focus too narrowly on their original target groups. "This year," they say, "we produced 100 bags of maize without outside help. We would welcome any assistance to set up schemes such as the rearing of poultry or pigs. The problem is that we have never met representatives of these organisations, we've never had any contact with them."

This indicates that there is potentially great popular support for VDF, and that it need only spread out more widely into other communities to consolidate the very useful work it has already done elsewhere. But, of course, VDF can only do as much as its finances allow.

And Chishimba stresses that, for the projects to have a significant impact, their managements should work closely with local government institutions. The projects should never be seen as competing with the work which government departments are doing, but rather as complementary to these efforts.

It is evident that VDF has achieved this and that it has successfully overcome the suspicions which it initially aroused. Indeed, it is probably therein that the main lesson from VDF's experience lies: that NGOs can be sound allies of the central government precisely because they get to the heart of the matter in ways which mobilise rural villagers to do things for themselves.

INDONESIA

ENDING THE DAILY
WATER CHORE

HARRY BHASKARA

INDONESIA: Ending the daily water chore

HARRY BHASKARA

The people of Kepuharjo village in Indonesia still remember their daily trudge to a mountain stream for water: four kilometres (2.5 miles) uphill, and four kilometres downhill carrying their load. The inescapable, unceasing, day after day chore drained their energy and cut down the time for cultivating their land.

At one stage, local officials urged them to improve their lives by raising cattle. But there was no water — except in the stream. They tried using bamboo pipes to bring the water, but it did not work.

Then, in 1971, a young engineering student, Anton Soedjarwo, came with a few friends and helped the people to lay pipes from the stream to communal taps in the village.

"Anton lived with us for one year and together we motivated people in three 'kampongs' (villages) — Kepuharjo, Glagaharjo and Umbulharjo," says Ngatmowagito, the 75-year-old head of Kepuharjo who led the water project committee. "Afterwards, for the next one and a half years, he came here every Wednesday to give lessons in agriculture."

The water project has transformed life in Kepuharjo, a village which is about 50 kilometres (30 miles) to the north of Yogyakarta on Indonesia's mainland, Java island. It is about 1,300 metres (4,250 feet) above sea level near Mount Merapi. The people traditionally depended on rain water for subsistence farming and harvested their crops once a year.

INDONESIA: Ending the daily water chore

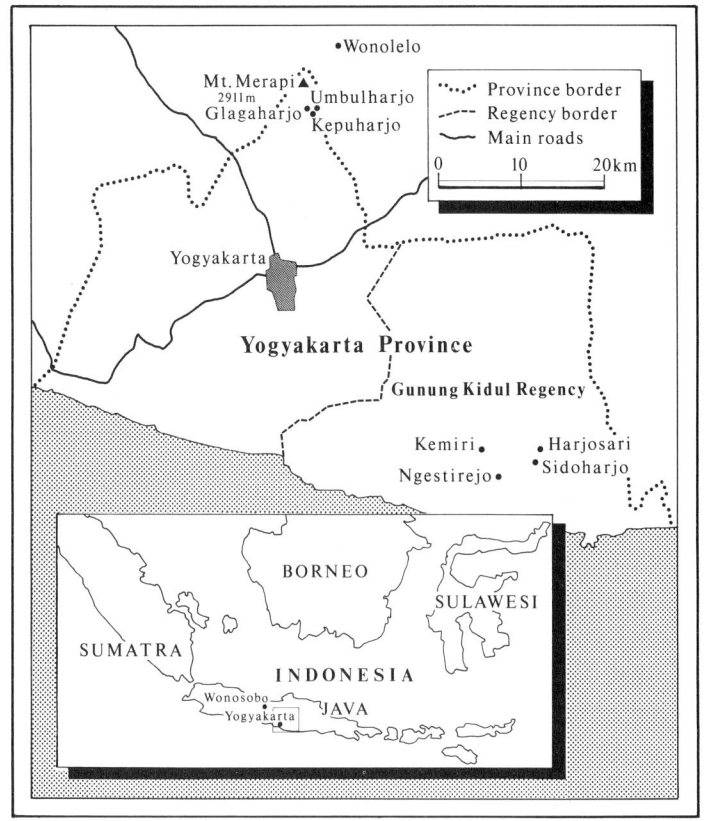

Yogyakarta province

"Now we can have two harvests in a year. Water has enabled us to cultivate our land all through the year," says Ngatmowagito.

A villager, Kasijo, says he takes a bath every day because water runs right into his house. "Before, we spent hours walking to take clean water from the spring." Now clean water flows in front of his house and he only has to connect a plastic tube to a concrete container to get it. "We use as much as we need," says the father of four children. "When we have enough in the house we simply disconnect the plastic tube."

One of the major accomplishments that went with the supply of water to the village was the construction of an 80-metre (260 feet)

AGAINST ALL ODDS

Dian Desa's water project has transformed the lives of people in Kepuharjo village.

iron pipe across a steep ravine which becomes a river in the rainy season. This is part of the main pipe connected from the spring to a water tank which flushes water, at the rate of about 60 litres per second, to supply the 2,300 people in Kepuharjo, the 3,000 in Glagaharjo and 3,000 in Umbulharjo.

"Villagers took part in the project," Ngatmowagito says. "I remember how they lifted the pipe. It needed 17 people to move each piece of the iron pipe."

It was not only the people in the three villages who benefited. For the success in bringing water to them and to others in the district motivated Anton Soedjarwo to set up Yayasan Dian Desa (Light of the Village Foundation).

He was then studying at the University of Gajah Mada in Yogyakarta. Now the director of Dian Desa, the soft-spoken Soedjarwo says in his office in Yogyakarta: "About 2 million people have been affected by the water supply programme."

> *'About 2 million people have been affected by the water supply programme.'*

Dian Desa's aim is to help overcome one of Indonesia's most pressing problems — the supply of clean water.

Indonesia — the unusual state

Indonesia is unlike any other state in the world: the largest archipelago, its 170 million people live on 17,508 islands sprawled across the equator. The population is unevenly distributed: Java has one of the highest population densities in the world with 640 people per square kilometre, while Borneo has fewer than 10 people per square kilometre.

Looking at the bare statistics, the country seems to have a plentiful supply of water: an average 18,846 cubic metres a year of potential water for each person, compared with the world average of 10,000 cubic metres. But, in practice, only about 30% is potable..

The rainfall figures are also deceptive, with some areas getting huge amounts of up to 700 centimetres (270 inches) a year; other parts get 70 centimetres (26 inches) a year. The average for the country is 267 centimetres (105 inches) a year.

By 1984 — the end of the third five-year development plan — the government was barely able to supply clean water to 30% of the rural population, despite the aid of the Dutch Government, the Asian Development Bank, and the United Nations. In terms of the 1984 population, clean water has to be provided in total for roughly 50,000 villages with some 27 million families. Assuming that Rupiahs 50,000 (about US$30) is needed for each family, then the funding required will be Rp1,350 billion (US$816 million) — or six times the 1983/1984 state budget for the health sector.

It is clear that the government alone will not be able to solve the water supply problem. Hence the repeated statements by leaders that the concerted efforts of both the government and the people are needed — which includes the helping hands of non-governmental organisations (NGOs).

Dian Desa— an early participant

Dian Desa was one of the earliest NGOs to immerse itself in the water problem. That initial small group of voluntary students has become an organisation with 120 staff. Their first work on the slopes of Mount Merapi has extended virtually across the country, covering 30 regencies (one regency contains 10 districts) in nine of the 27 provinces.

Although Dian Desa's chief focus is to help with the provision of water, it has found it necessary to broaden its scope. The organisation is now divided into nine sections: water supply, agriculture and fisheries, food technology, energy, small-scale industry, workshop, social work, publication and library.

Why this became necessary is seen in Kepuharjo: in addition to the water project, Dian Desa introduced the villagers to the growing of clove trees and the generation of biogas energy. The clove trees were aimed at increasing incomes so that villagers could afford to maintain the water pipe in good condition. The biogas project was intended to change the villagers' habit of cutting down trees for fuelwood.

However, says village head Ngatmowagito: "The energy programme was not successful because villagers feel that making energy from animals' manure is too complicated. Besides, they knew that unused dried tree branches were abundant."

On the other hand, he notes that there has been a significant improvement in the village's life since Dian Desa began working there: "Not only our income increased but our whole village changed. Villagers could afford to improve their houses."

"Through the water project the villagers have recovered their self-confidence," says Anton Soedjarwo. "At one point there were some 300 people working on the iron water pipe above the ravine. It is important to maintain this fire of confidence. If, before, they thought they were incapable of growing healthy vegetables because there were no seeds, now they believe they can do it. This kind of thing, the self-confidence, is something we cannot measure in money."

The water-starved past

In the village of Kemiri, in the Gunung Kidul regency, Hadi Sutrisno remembers the water-starved past: when he was a child his father had to walk 14 kilometres (nearly 9 miles) to fetch water: "He had to walk from early morning and did not come back home until three o'clock in the afternoon. Now it has changed. More and more people help us with the supply of water."

Significant progress has been made to help ease the chronic shortage of water in Gunung Kidul. The dry range of mountains 56 kilometres (35 miles) east of Yogyakarta has 18 districts and 144 villages. News of drought from this regency hits newspaper headlines every year. In the latest dry season, some 40 villages with 28,000 families and 143,000 people suffered the effects of severe drought.

This represented about 20% of Gunung Kidul's population. Nearly all 289 natural water catchment ponds in the regency were dry. In the most stricken districts, the helpless villagers depended on irregular deliveries by government water tank trucks.

The villagers — mostly poor — had to buy the water for Rp50

(3US cents) per 40 litres. It has become a tradition that in such conditions private charities donate water to the region.

Gunung Kidul is one of the areas where Dian Desa organised a water catchment tank project with the assistance of the Ministry of Health and the United Nations Children's Fund (UNICEF). The ministry calculated that Gunung Kidul, which is largely deforested and ground water virtually non-existent, needs about 30,000 catchment tanks. However, according to Verry Renyaan, head of the water section at Dian Desa, thus far it has only about 20,000 — which includes 6,000 ferro-cement tanks and 3,000 bamboo-cement tanks constructed by villagers with Dian Desa support.

> *'He had to walk from early morning and did not come back home until three o'clock in the afternoon. Now it has changed.'*

In Harjosari village in the Gunung Kidul regency, villagers queue for water once every two days at a government water storage tank.

"If there is no water I have to take water from Mulo subterranean cave about four kilometres from here," says Harjomuhadi as he waits his turn to get water from the tank. His bamboo-cement tank in front of his house has broken. "It was broken after six years of use. A ferro-cement tank is stronger but I do not have the money yet to make one," he says.

Bamboo-cement tanks are designed to last up to seven years, while a ferro-cement tank can last for 25 years.

For how long can a catchment tank provide water in the dry season? "One and a half months," says Harjomuhadi. "The water is consumed by my family and my neighbours."

The tanks for 'last resort'

The Dian Desa tanks are meant for the "last resort" use of water — an important aspect often overlooked by villagers.

In Sidoharjo village, in the same regency, the project gave rise

INDONESIA: Ending the daily water chore

The supply of clean water is one of Indonesia's most pressing problems; people trudge long distances every day to collect water.

to an unexpected side-effect: "Villagers fill their tanks with water from the nearby Jurug pond. This caused the 80-year-old man-made pond to dry up faster than it usually does," says Mangun Suwardi, Sidoharjo's village head.

There are 60 Dian Desa tanks in this village: 90% of the bamboo-cement tanks have been out of order, but only 10% of the ferro-cement tanks need repair. "Almost all of the tanks were built and financed by the villagers themselves," says the village head. He notes that about 10% of the 6,000 population still want to build Dian Desa tanks as soon as they can afford to make one.

Properly constructed bamboo-cement tanks can last longer than the specified age. One such tank belongs to S. Hadi, who is secretary of the adjoining Ngestirejo village. At the back of his modest house he has both ferro- and bamboo-cement tanks. Clean water runs well as Hadi turns on the taps of both tanks. "The bamboo- cement tank is eight years old. Except for little leaks here and there it is still good," he says. "Those bamboo tanks that have already broken must have been built carelessly. Some villagers were not careful enough when they made the tanks."

The Dian Desa project benefits the village, he says: "Compared with the difficult years in the 1950s, we can say that water is no longer a problem now."

A villager, met while taking a bath in a pond between Ngestirejo and Sidoharjo villages, says some villagers have to drink the brackish water from the pond. "But I never use it for drinking water because I have a Dian Desa tank at home," he says.

The enduring problem

But Gunung Kidul has enduring problems. There is very little good soil and this makes it difficult for the villagers to disentangle themselves from poverty. Apart from subsistence farming, villagers raise cattle to earn their living.

"In my opinion our programme at Gunung Kidul has not achieved its target," says Harry Susanto, a Dian Desa staffer who virtually lived there from 1980 to 1985, "because from the beginning we made a mistake in choosing the recipients. We selected the poorest among the poor. The result is that those who can afford to make their own tank do not make one but take water from their less affluent neighbours."

Dian Desa classifies those who have cows and a sizeable amount of land as financially capable of making their own water catchment tank. On the technical side, he says villagers often neglect instructions to use well-dried bamboo: "They use a young bamboo tree inbetween the dried and mature bamboo plaits. If one plait of the frame contains a younger bamboo then the whole tank will crack in a short time."

That this observation is correct is demonstrated because Hadi's own bamboo frame tank is still functioning. "Occasionally people are not careful enough in installing the bamboo frame," he explains. "They put it too low on the basement cement of the container. It

INDONESIA: Ending the daily water chore

should be located at some distance from the floor. Moreover, the bamboo is sometimes not woven carefully."

Water: the key to the programmes

"We view the water project as an integrated programme," says Verry Renyaan, the Dian Desa staffer. "Water is the key to other programmes. We cannot talk about growing trees in house-yards, for instance, or income-generating, in those villages that have no water."

Thus some villages have no potential to go ahead. But if they prove they do, they are offered income-generating programmes — on condition that they share with Dian Desa.

This is the product-sharing scheme, aimed at further boosting villagers' self-confidence in improving their lot. By sharing their products with Dian Desa, villagers are rid of feeling that they are

Ferro-cement tanks, as shown here, last longer than those constructed with bamboo and cement.

wholly dependent on others for progress. This feeling was rampant among Dian Desa recipients in the earlier period and was closely related to the waning of their fighting spirit.

Dian Desa recycles the products received from villagers to help finance projects in other villages and also to fund its own staff in the field so that the organisation can be more independent. After two or four years, Dian Desa leaves projects entirely in the hands of the villagers. By this time it is expected that they will have the required skill and confidence to progress on their own.

"Blabak villagers in Wonolelo district, for instance, contribute a certain percentage of funds on every harvest for Dian Desa," explains Renyaan. "It is a revolving plan. We assist other villages with those funds."

> *'We cannot talk about growing trees in house-yards, for instance, or income-generating in those villages that have no water.'*

Don't villagers complain about the funds they raise being given to other villages? "No, we use different approaches, for instance talking with a community leader, such as the 'kiai' (religious leader) in the villages. In Wonosobo, Central Java, the kiai preached that helping people in other villages was in line with the teaching of religion.

"That is what we mean by an integrated programme. We cannot view it as a separate programme but see it as a starting-point for other programmes. That's our philosophy. In this way I believe we can answer the water problem in other villages."

Strongwilled villagers

The determination to improve living standards is obvious among villagers in the district. Blabak village, for example, which lies about 60 kilometres (37 miles) to the northeast of Yogyakarta and more than 1,000 metres (3,250 feet) above sea level, is endowed with fertile land and strongwilled people.

Village head Siwo Nuryanto was the winner of the 1980 Kalpataru environment award from the government: he was

INDONESIA: Ending the daily water chore

Although Indonesia has a plentiful supply of water, only about 30% is fit for drinking.

credited for his success in bringing water from mountain streams to houses of the 4,500 villagers.

After the water problem was solved, villagers wanted water for their plantations. In 1983, Dian Desa, with the assistance of a Canadian organisation, built a concrete system to supply about 40 families. The product-sharing scheme is now underway in the village. This scheme has now spread to five other villages in the area.

Nuryanto says the villagers are very happy with the income-generating programme: "We learnt a lot from Dian Desa. Before we did not know how to grow garlic; now more and more villagers are improving their skills to grow this crop."

Dian Desa introduced a short-range programme of two years, and a long-range one of five years for the villagers. The villagers decided for themselves which programme they wanted.

"We give half of our harvest to Dian Desa and feel that is very justifiable considering the guidance and knowledge we gain," says Nuryanto.

There are two reasons why Dian Desa has been switching from straight-out charity, explains Kris Bandono of Dian Desa. The first is experience gathered in the field that charity weakens the villagers' drive to attain self-help. He cites the credit system used in Gunung Kidul, known as the "goat" project: villagers who cannot afford to make water tanks are given a goat for breeding, when the goat multiplies, the owner gets one goat for himself to be sold and the money used to build the tank.

"What happens, however, is that the goat we give them remains small and never multiplies. We found out that, as soon as the goat gets bigger, they change it in the market for a smaller one; they keep doing this to earn extra money from the swap."

From villagers to slum dwellers

Dian Desa also works in the cities. An example is the handpump water project initiated in 1986 to provide clean water to slum dwellers in the city of Yogyakarta. The polyvinyl chloride (PVC) pump is designed for village use and has a manual so simple that an illiterate user can install the pump and make minor repairs.

Similar to the product-sharing scheme, the pump project is partly subsidised and users pay Rp50,000 (US$30) in instalments over two years. This is 40% of the actual price.

Dian Desa was responsible for investigating the social acceptability of the pump and its technical performance.

Slum dwellers in Yogyakarta can usually afford to buy modern electronic equipment like TV sets and radios. "If they can buy these things they must also be able to buy a water pump," notes Christina Aristanti Sujarwo, Dian Desa's assistant director who heads the project.

Within only a year Dian Desa installed 120 pumps in 16 locations, including slum areas and villages.

INDONESIA: Ending the daily water chore

'The projects provide a focus for the community.'

As soon as the slum dwellers in Kricak Kidul, Sidomulyo and Gemblekan Bawah in the vicinity of Yogyakarta had their handpumps in place, they proposed that Dian Desa arrange a toilet project with similar instalment arrangements as the handpump project. "To my surprise I learnt that slum dwellers have a high health consciousness and a strong independent attitude," says Sujarwo.

However, the government's 40% devaluation of the rupiah in 1986 had an adverse effect on the project. "The price skyrocketed to about Rp150,000 (US$90) after the devaluation and prospective users were shocked to learn what it would cost them," she says.

"If the handpump remains at Rp50,000 every person in my

Villagers are no longer dependent on outside sources for one of their most basic needs: water.

village would want one," says Sugimo, who lives in Mangunan village, about 15 kilometres from Yogyakarta. And even with the price increase, at least 50 people in the village still applied for the pump.

The pump's underground equipment is imported from Malaysia, and Dian Desa supplies only the above-ground equipment. Notes Christina Sujarwo: "That is why we are thinking of the possibility of local production with the primary intention of lowering the price." Indeed, efforts to make PVC pumps locally are already under way. A pump developed at Dian Desa's workshop costs only Rp20,000 (US$12) to produce. But further experiments are needed before it can be ready for use.

Dian Desa offers three types of ownership of the pump: individual, group, or public. Most slum dwellers have opted for individual ownership.

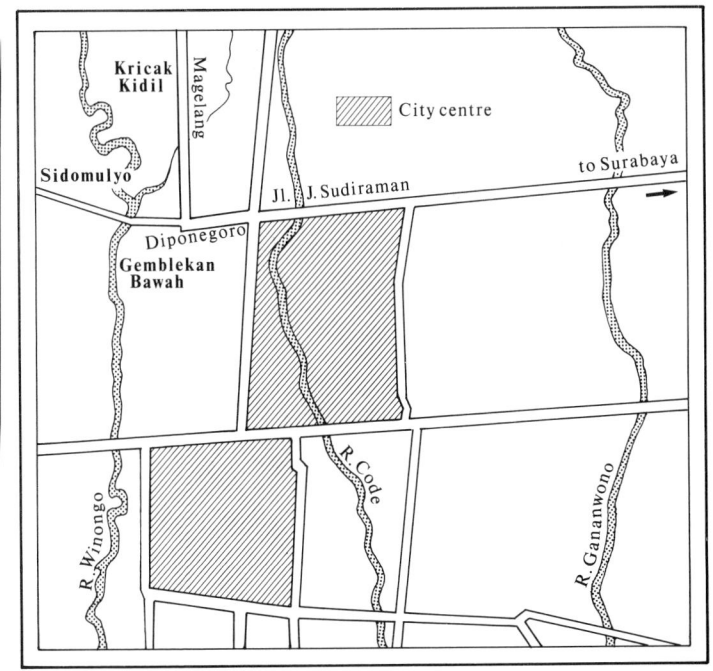

Yogyakarta City

A careful, sympathetic approach

Supplying water is one of the earliest of Yayasan Dian Desa projects. It dates back about 20 years and affects about 2 million people who are mostly villagers.

Over the years the character of the project has changed, from being more of a charity into a programme which takes into account the ability of villagers to improve their living standard.

Villages vary from one to another: some have agricultural potential and a degree of high solidarity, and others do not. Through its long experience, Dian Desa and its staff have gained understanding of village problems.

> *'I never believe in remote control ... We use a careful and sympathetic approach by living with the villagers.'*

"I never believe in remote control," says Anton Soedjarwo. "We use a careful and sympathetic approach by living with the villagers and trying to understand their problems as one of them."

He stresses, too, that Dian Desa always works hand in hand with the government in its various projects: "Who are the government and who are we but people who have the same objective? If there happen to be some difficulties in working together it means that we still have weaknesses to communicate."

Dian Desa's activities continue to develop. Water will make villagers' lives healthier and more enjoyable but it does not automatically increase their income. After their basic needs have been fulfilled, Dian Desa is ready with its follow-up projects.

"The water we are talking about is water which exists," says Soedjarwo. In some locations it has to be procured from a distance, but the water is there. In other places, however, water resources are non-existent. In such cases must not misuse this precious natural resouce.

"Our philosophy is partnership. Those who are willing to look for ways to overcome their own problems can get our assistance through appropriate technology."

If you would like further information please contact:

INDIA: The pavement dwellers of Bombay
Society for Promotion of Area Resource Centres (SPARC),
Meghraj Sethi Marg,
Municipal Dispensary, Byculla,
Bombay 400 008, India

TANZANIA: A life-saving clinic in remote Chanika
Community Development Trust Fund (CDTF),
PO Box 9421,
Dar es Salaam, Tanzania

BANGLADESH: Breaking the grip of greedy landowners
Executive Director,
Proshika Manobik Unnayan Kendra,
5/2 Iqbal Road, Mohammadpur,
Dhaka 2, Bangladesh

KENYA: The parking boys of Nairobi
UNDUGU Society,
PO Box 40417,
Nairobi, Kenya

INDIA: No longer need they abandon home
Project Director,
Uthanmanik Project,
MAHITI,
83/387 Saraswati Nagar,
Ahmedabad, India

KENYA: The water that brings new life
Kenya Water for Health Organisation,
PO Box 61470,
Nairobi, Kenya

SRI LANKA: Growing trees in the light of the Buddha
Nation Builders Association,
48 Hill Street,
Mahanuwara,
Kandy, Sri Lanka

ZAMBIA: The same hands, but new minds
Village Development Foundation,
PO Box 113, Mungwi,
Kasama, Zambia

INDONESIA: Ending the daily water chore
Yayasan Dian Desa,
Jl. Kaliurang Km.7,
PO Box 19, Bulaksumur,
Yogyakarta, Central Java,
Indonesia